Helping Worriers

Helping Worriers

James R. Beck
and David T. Moore

Baker Books
A Division of Baker Book House Co
Grand Rapids, Michigan 49516

©1994 by James R. Beck and David T. Moore

Published by Baker Books,
a division of Baker Book House Company
P.O. Box 6287
Grand Rapids, Michigan 49516-6287

Printed in the United States of America

Library of Congress Cataloging-in-Publication Data

Beck, James R.
    Helping worriers / James R. Beck and David T. Moore.
        p.   cm. — (Strategic pastoral counseling resources)
    Includes bibliographical references.
    ISBN 0-8010-1084-5
    1. Pastoral counseling. 2. Worry—Religious aspects—Christianity.
I. Moore, David T. II. Title. III Series.
    BV4012.2.B35   1994
    253.5—dc20   94-20700

Contents

Preface

We tried not to worry as we were writing this book. But try as we might, our human natures seemed to push us toward worry more than we liked. Writing a book about such a common human struggle really means that we are writing about ourselves as well as other worriers. Now that the project is complete we know more about how to deal with our own worry. We continue to plug away at keeping it under reasonable control.

We wrote this book during the summer of 1993 while residing in two very different settings. Jim worked on the project while living on a family farm in waterlogged Kansas on his academic sabbatical. The rains and floods qualified as the every 100 years variety. Farmer friends and neighbors agonized as they watched ripe crops sit in fields too muddy for the harvesting machinery. Crop values fell each day the overripe wheat sat with its roots in mud. Did the farmers worry? Of course they did; some more than others.

Meanwhile, Dave worked on the project while carrying out his summer pastoring duties in fabled southern California. His portions were written in the midst of a summer schedule that included 80 different speaking engagements!

We have written this book to help pastors who serve people like Kansas farmers and California Boomers. Our prayer is that this material will enrich and enliven your counseling ministries to the worriers in your congregation, and perhaps to your personal life as well.

JRB
DTM

7

An Introduction to Strategic Pastoral Counseling

David G. Benner

While the provision of spiritual counsel has been an integral part of Christian soul care since the earliest days of the church, the contemporary understanding and practice of pastoral counseling is largely a product of the twentieth century. Developing within the shadow of the modern psychotherapies, pastoral counseling has derived much of its style and approach from these clinical therapeutics. What this has meant is that pastoral counselors have often seen themselves more as counselors than as pastors, and the counseling that they have provided has often been a rather awkward adaptation of clinical counseling models to a pastoral context. This, in turn, has often resulted in significant tension between the pastoral and psychological dimensions of the counseling provided by clergy and others in Christian ministry. It is also frequently reflected in pastoral counselors who are more interested in anything connected with the modern mystery cult of psychotherapy than with their own tradition of Christian soul care, and who, as a consequence, are often quite insecure in their pastoral role and identity.

While pastoral counseling owes much to the psychological culture that has gained ascendancy in the West during the past century, this influence has quite clearly been a mixed blessing. Con-

9

temporary pastoral counselors typically offer their help with much more psychological sophistication than was the case several decades ago, but all too often they do so without a clear sense of the uniqueness of counseling that is offered by a pastor. And not only are the distinctive spiritual resources of Christian ministry often deemphasized or ignored, but the tensions that are associated with attempts to directly translate clinical models of counseling into the pastoral context become a source of much frustration. This is in part why so many pastors report dissatisfaction with their counseling. While they indicate that this dissatisfaction is a result of insufficient training in and time for counseling, a bigger part of the problem may be that pastors have been offered approaches to counseling that are of questionable appropriateness for the pastoral context and that will inevitably leave them frustrated and feeling inadequate.

Strategic Pastoral Counseling is a model of counseling that has been specifically designed to fit the role, resources, and needs of the typical pastor who counsels. Information about this "typical" pastor was solicited by means of a survey of over 400 pastors; this research is described in the introductory volume to the series, *Strategic Pastoral Counseling: An Overview* (Benner, 1992). The model appropriates the insights of contemporary counseling theory without sacrificing the resources of pastoral ministry. Furthermore, it takes its form and direction from the pastoral role and in so doing offers an approach to counseling that is not only congruent with the other aspects of pastoral ministry, but which places pastoral counseling at the very heart of ministry.

The present volume represents an application of Strategic Pastoral Counseling to one commonly encountered problem situation. As such, it presupposes a familiarity with the basic model. Readers not familiar with *Strategic Pastoral Counseling: An Overview* should consult this book for a detailed presentation of the model and its implementation. What follows is a brief review of this material that, while it does not adequately summarize all that is presented in that book, should serve as a reminder of the most important features of the Strategic Pastoral Counseling approach.

The Strategic Pastoral Counseling Model

Strategic Pastoral Counseling is short-term, bibliotherapeutic, wholistic, structured, spiritually focused, and explicitly Christian. Each of these characteristics will be briefly discussed in order.

Short-Term Counseling

Counseling can be brief (that is, conducted over a relatively few sessions), or time-limited (that is, conducted within an initially fixed number of total sessions), or both. Strategic Pastoral Counseling is both brief and time-limited, working within a suggested maximum of five sessions. The decision to set this upper limit on the number of sessions was a response to the fact that the background research conducted in the design of the model indicated that 87 percent of the pastoral counseling conducted by pastors in general ministry involves five sessions or less. This short-term approach to counseling seems ideally suited to the time, availability, training, and role demands of pastors.

Recent research in short-term counseling has made it clear that while such an approach requires that the counselor be diligent in maintaining the focus on the single agreed upon central problem, significant and enduring changes can occur through a very small number of counseling sessions. Strategic Pastoral Counseling differs, in this regard, from the more ongoing relationship of discipleship or spiritual guidance. In these, the goal is the development of spiritual maturity. Strategic Pastoral Counseling has a much more modest goal: namely, examining a particular problem or experience in the light of God's will for, and activity in, the life of the individual seeking help, then attempting to facilitate that person's growth in and through his or her present life situation. While this is still an ambitious goal, its focused nature makes it quite attainable within a short period of time. It is this focus that makes the counseling strategic.

The five-session limit should be communicated by the pastor no later than the first session and preferably in the prior conversation when the time was set for the first. This ensures that the parishioner is aware of the time limit from the beginning and can share responsibility in keeping the counseling sessions focused. Some people will undoubtedly require more than five sessions in order to bring about a resolution of their problems. These people should be referred to someone who is appropriately qualified for such work. Preparation for this referral will be one of the goals of the five sessions. However, the fact that such people may require more than can be provided in five sessions of pastoral counseling does not mean that they cannot benefit from such focused short-term pastoral care and no one should be seen to be inappropriate for Strategic Pastoral Counseling merely because they may also require other help.

One final but important note about the suggested limit of five sessions is that this does not have to be tied to a corresponding period of five weeks. In fact, many pastors find weekly sessions to be less useful than sessions scheduled two or three weeks apart. This sort of spacing of the last couple of sessions is particularly helpful and should be considered even if the first several sessions are held weekly.

Bibliotherapeutic Counseling

Bibliotherapy refers to the therapeutic use of reading, and Strategic Pastoral Counseling builds the use of written materials into the heart of its approach to pastoral care giving. The Bible itself is, of course, a rich bibliotherapeutic resource, and the encouragement of and direction in its reading is an important part of Strategic Pastoral Counseling. Its use must be disciplined and selective and particular care must be taken to ensure that it is never employed in a mechanical or impersonal manner. However, when used appropriately, it can unquestionably be one of the most dynamic and powerful resources available to the pastor who counsels.

But while the Bible is a unique bibliotherapeutic resource, it is not the only such resource. Strategic Pastoral Counseling comes with a built-in set of specifically designed resources. Each of the ten volumes in this series has an accompanying book written for the parishioner who is being seen in counseling. These resource books are written by the same authors as the volume for pastors and are designed for easy integration into the counseling.

The use of reading materials that are consistent with the counseling being provided can serve as a most significant support and extension of the counseling offered by a pastor. The parishioner now has a helping resource that is not limited by the pastor's time and availability. Furthermore, the pastor can now allow the written materials to do part of the work of counseling, using the sessions to deal with those matters that are not as well addressed through the written page.

Wholistic Counseling

It might seem surprising to suggest that a counseling approach that is short-term should also be wholistic, but this is both possible and highly desirable. Wholistic counseling is counseling that is responsive to the totality of the complex psychospiritual dynamics that make up the life of human persons. Biblical psychology is clearly a wholistic psychology. The various "parts" of persons (i.e., body, soul, spirit, heart, flesh, etc.) are never presented as separate faculties or independent components of persons, but always as different ways of seeing the whole person. Biblical discussions of persons emphasize first and foremost our essential unity of being. Humans are ultimately understandable only in the light of this primary and irreducible wholeness, and helping efforts that are truly Christian must resist the temptation to see persons only through their thoughts, feelings, behaviors, or any one other manifestation of being.

The alternative to wholism in counseling is to focus on only one of these modalities of functioning, and this is what many approaches to counseling do. In contrast to this, Strategic Pastoral Counseling asserts that pastoral counseling must be responsive to the behavioral (action), cognitive (thought), and affective (feeling) elements of personal functioning. Each examined separately can obscure that which is really going on with a person. But taken together, they form the basis for a comprehensive assessment and effective intervention. Strategic Pastoral Counseling provides a framework for ensuring that each of these spheres of functioning is addressed, and this, in fact, provides much of the structure for the counseling.

Structured Counseling

The structured nature of Strategic Pastoral Counseling is that which enables its brevity, the structure ensuring that each of the sessions has a clear focus and that each builds upon the previous ones in contributing toward the accomplishment of the overall goals. The framework that structures Strategic Pastoral Counseling is sufficiently tight as to enable the pastor to provide a wholistic assessment and counseling intervention within a maximum of five sessions; yet it is also sufficiently flexible to allow for differences in individual styles of different counselors. This is very important because Strategic Pastoral Counseling is not primarily a set of techniques but is an intimate encounter of and dialogue between two people.

The structure of Strategic Pastoral Counseling grows out of the goal of addressing the feelings, thoughts, and behaviors that are a part of the troubling experiences of the person seeking help. It is also a structure that is responsive to the several tasks that face the pastoral counselor, tasks such as conducting an initial assessment, developing a general understanding of the problem and of the person's major needs, and selecting and delivering interventions and resources that will bring help. This structure is described in more detail later.

Spiritually Focused Counseling

The fourth distinctive of Strategic Pastoral Counseling is that it is spiritually focused. This does not mean that only religious matters are discussed. Our spirituality is our essential heart commitments, our basic life direction, and our fundamental allegiances. These spiritual aspects of our being are, of course, reflected in our attitudes toward God and are expressed in our explicitly religious values and behaviors. However, they are also reflected in matters that may seem on the surface to be much less religious. Strategic Pastoral Counselors place a primacy on listening to this underlying spiritual story. They listen for what we might call the story behind the story.

But listening to the story behind the story requires that one first listen to and take seriously the presenting story. To disregard the presenting situation is spiritualization of a problem. It fails to take the problem seriously and makes a mockery of counseling as genuine dialogue. The Strategic Pastoral Counselor thus listens to and enters into the experience of parishioners as they relate their struggles and life experiences. While this is a real part of the story, it is not the whole story that must be heard and understood. For in the midst of this story emerges another, the story of their spiritual response to these experiences. This response may be one of unwavering trust in God, but a failure to expect much of him. Or it may be one of doubt, anger, confusion, or despair. Each of these are spiritual responses to present struggles, and in one form or another, the spiritual aspect of the person's experience will always be discernible to the pastor who watches for it. The Strategic Pastoral Counseling makes this underlying spiritual story the primary focus.

Explicitly Christian Counseling

But while it is important to not confuse spirituality with religiosity, it is equally important to not confuse Christian spirituality with any of its imitations. In this regard, it is crucial that Strategic Pastoral Counseling be distinctively and explicitly Christian. While Strategic Pastoral Counseling begins with a focus on spiritual matters understood broadly, its master goal is to facilitate the other person's awareness of and response to the call of God to surrender and service. This is the essential and most important distinctive of Strategic Pastoral Counseling.

One of the ways in which Strategic Pastoral Counseling is made explicitly Christian is through its utilization of Christian theological language, images, and concepts and the religious resources of prayer, Scriptures, and the sacraments. As pointed out earlier, these resources must never be used in a mechanical, legalistic, or magical fashion. Used sensitively and wisely, they can be the conduit for a dynamic contact between God and the person seeking pastoral help. The goal of their utilization is not some superficial baptizing of the counseling in order to make it Christian, but rather, a way of bringing the one seeking help more closely in touch with the God who is the source of all life, growth, and healing.

Another important resource that is appropriated by the Strategic Pastoral Counselor is that of the church as a community. Too often pastoral counseling is conducted in a way that is not appreciably different from that which might be offered by a Christian counselor in private practice. This most unfortunate practice ignores the rich resources that are potentially available in any Christian congregation. One of the most important ways to maintain the short-term nature of Strategic Pastoral Counseling is to have the pastor connect the person seeking help with others in the church who can provide portions of that help. The congregation can, of course, also be involved in less individualistic ways. Support and ministry groups of various sorts are becoming a part of many congregations that seek to provide a dynamic ministry to their community, and are important potential resources for the Strategic Pastoral Counselor.

A final and even more fundamental way in which Strategic Pastoral Counseling is Christian is in the reliance on the Holy Spirit that it encourages. The Spirit is the indispensable source of all wisdom that is necessary for the practice of pastoral counseling. Recognizing that all healing and growth is ultimately of God, the Strategic Pastoral Counselor can thus take comfort in a reliance on the Spirit of God, and on the fact that ultimate responsibility for counselees and their well-being lies with God.

Stages and Tasks of Strategic Pastoral Counseling

The three overall stages that organize Strategic Pastoral Counseling can be described as Encounter, Engagement, and Disengagement. The first stage of Strategic Pastoral Counseling, Encounter, corresponds to the initial session. The goal is to establish a personal contact with the person seeking help, to set the boundaries for the counseling relationship, to become acquainted with the individual and his or her central concerns, to conduct a pastoral diagnosis, and to develop a mutually acceptable focus for the subsequent sessions. The second stage, Engagement, involves the pastor moving beyond the first contact and establishing a deeper working alliance with the person seeking help. This normally occupies the next one to three sessions. It entails the exploration of the person's feelings, thoughts, and behavioral patterns associated with this problem area, and the development of new perspectives and strategies for coping or change. The third and final stage, Disengagement, describes the focus of the last one or possibly two sessions. These involve an evaluation of progress and an assessment of remaining concerns, the making of a referral for further help if needed, and the ending of the counseling relationship. These stages and tasks are summarized below.

Stages and Tasks of Strategic Pastoral Counseling

Stage 1: Encounter (Session 1)
- Joining and boundary setting
- Exploring the central concerns and relevant history
- Conducting a pastoral diagnosis
- Achieving a mutually agreeable focus for counseling

Stage 2: Engagement (Sessions 2, 3, and 4)
- Exploration of cognitive, affective, and behavioral aspects of the problem and the identification of resources for coping or change

Stage 3: Disengagement (Sessions 4 and 5)
- Evaluation of progress and assessment of remaining concerns
- Referral (if needed)
- Termination of counseling

The Encounter Stage

The first task in this initial stage of Strategic Pastoral Counseling is joining and boundary setting. Joining involves putting the parishioner at ease by means of a few moments of casual conversation that is designed to ease pastor and parishioner into contact. Such preliminary conversation should never take more than five minutes and should usually be kept to two or three. It will not always be necessary, some people being immediately ready to tell their story. Boundary setting involves the communication of the purpose of a session, of the time frame for the session and your work together. This should not normally require more than a sentence or two.

The exploration of central concerns and relevant history usually begins with an invitation for the parishioner to describe what led him or her to seek help at the present time. After hearing these immediate concerns, it is usually helpful to get a brief historical perspective on these concerns and the person. Ten to fifteen minutes of exploration into the development of the problems and the individual's efforts to cope or get help with them is the foundation of this part of the session. It is also important at this point to get some idea of the parishioner's present living and family arrangements, as well as his or her work or educational situation. The organizing thread for this section of the first interview should be the presenting problem. It will not be the only matter discussed, but this focus serves to give the session the necessary direction.

Stripped of its distracting medical connotations, diagnosis is problem definition, and this is a fundamental part of any approach to counseling. Diagnoses involve judgments about the nature of the problem and, either implicitly or explicitly, pastoral counselors make such judgments every time they commence a counseling relationship. However, in order for diagnoses to be relevant, they must guide the counseling that will follow. This means that the categories of pastoral assessment must be primarily related to the spiritual focus that is foundational to any counseling that is appropriately called pastoral. Thus, the diagnosis that is called for in the first stage of Strategic Pastoral Counseling involves an assessment of the person's spiritual well-being.

The framework for pastoral diagnosis adopted by Strategic Pastoral Counseling is that suggested by Malony (1988) and used as the basis of his *Religious Status Interview*. Malony proposed that the diagnosis of Christian religious well-being should involve the assessment of the person's awareness of God, acceptance of God's grace, repentance and responsibility, response to God's leadership and direction, involvement in the church, experience of fellowship, ethics, and openness in faith. While this approach to pastoral diagnosis has been found to be helpful by many, the Strategic Pastoral Counselor need not feel confined by it. It is offered as a suggested framework for conducting a pastoral assessment, and each pastoral counselor needs to approach this task in ways that fit his or her own theological convictions and personal style. Further details on the conduct of a pastoral assessment can be found in *Strategic Pastoral Counseling: An Overview* (Benner, 1992).

The final task of the Encounter stage is achieving a mutually agreeable focus for counseling. Often this is self-evident, made immediately clear by the first expression of the parishioner. At other times parishioners will report a wide range of concerns in the first session and will have to be asked what should constitute the primary problem focus. The identification of the primary problem focus leads naturally to a formulation of goals for the counseling. These goals will sometimes be quite specific (e.g., to be able to make an informed decision about a potential job change) but will also at times be rather broad (e.g., to be able to express my feelings related to an illness). As is illustrated in these examples, some goals will describe an endpoint while others will describe more of a process. Maintaining this flexibility in how goals are understood is crucial if Strategic Pastoral Counseling is to be a helpful counseling approach for the broad range of situations faced by the pastoral counselor.

The Engagement Stage

The second stage of Strategic Pastoral Counseling involves the further engagement of the pastor and the one seeking help around the problems and concerns that brought them together. This is the heart of the counseling process. The major tasks of this stage are the exploration of the person's feelings, thoughts, and behavioral patterns associated with the central concerns and the development of new perspectives and strategies for coping or change.

It is important to note that the work of this stage may well begin in the first session. The model should not be interpreted in a rigid or mechanical manner. If the goals of the first stage are completed with time remaining in the first session, one can very appropriately begin to move into the tasks of this next stage. However, once the tasks of stage one are completed, those associated with this second stage become the central focus. If the full five sessions of Strategic Pastoral Counseling are employed, this second stage normally provides the structure for sessions two, three, and four.

The central foci for the three sessions normally associated with this stage are respectively the feelings, thoughts, and behaviors associated with the problem presented by the person seeking help. Although these are usually intertwined, a selective focus on each, one at a time, ensures that each is adequately addressed and that all the crucial dynamics of the person's psychospiritual functioning are considered.

The reason for beginning with feelings is that this is where most people themselves begin when they come to a counselor, but this does not mean that most people know their feelings. The exploration of feelings involves encouraging the person to face and express whatever it is that they are feeling, to the end that these feelings can be known and then dealt with appropriately. The goal at this point is to listen and respond emphatically to the feelings of the one seeking help, not to try to change them.

After an exploration of the major feelings being experienced by the person seeking help, the next task is an exploration of the thoughts associated with these feelings and the development of alternative ways of understanding present experiences. It is in this phase of Strategic Pastoral Counseling that the explicit use of Scriptures is usually most appropriate. Bearing in mind the potential misuses and problems that can be associated with such use of religious resources, the pastoral counselor should be, nonetheless, open to a direct presentation of scriptural truths when they offer the possibility of a new and helpful perspective on one's situation.

The final task of the Engagement stage of Strategic Pastoral Counseling grows directly out of this work on understanding and involves the exploration of the behavioral components of the person's functioning. Here the pastor explores what concrete things the person is doing in the face of the problems or distressing situations being encountered, and together with the parishioner begins to identify changes in behavior that may be desirable. The goal of this stage is to identify changes that both pastor and parishioner agree are important and to begin to establish concrete strategies for making these changes.

The Disengagement Stage

The last session or two involves preparation for the termination of counseling and includes two specific tasks: the evaluation of progress and assessment of remaining concerns, and making arrangements regarding a referral if necessary.

The evaluation of progress is usually a process that both pastor and parishioner will find to be rewarding. Some of this may be done during previous sessions, but even when this is the case, it is a good idea to use the last session to review what has been learned from the counseling. Closely associated with this, of course, is an identification of remaining concerns. Seldom is everything resolved after five sessions. This means that the parishioner is preparing to leave counseling with some work yet to be done, but he or she does so with plans for the future, and the development of these is an important task of the Disengagement stage of Strategic Pastoral Counseling.

If significant problems remain at this point, the last couple of sessions should also be used to make referral arrangements. Ideally these should be discussed in the second or third session, and they should by now be all arranged. It might even be ideal if by this point the parishioner has had a first session with the person whom he or she will be seeing, thus allowing a processing of the first experience as part of the final pastoral counseling session.

Recognition of one's own limitations of time, experience, training, and ability is an indispensable component of the practice of all professionals. Pastors are no exception. Pastors offering Strategic Pastoral Counseling need, therefore, to be aware of the resources within their community and be prepared to refer parishioners for help elsewhere.

In the vast majority of cases, the actual termination of a Strategic Pastoral Counseling relationship goes very smoothly. Most often both pastor and parishioner agree that there is no further need to meet, and they find easy agreement with, even if some sadness around, the decision to discontinue the counseling sessions. However, there may be times when this process is somewhat difficult. This will sometimes be due to the parishioner's desire to continue to meet. At other times the difficulty in terminating will reside within the pastor. Regardless, the best course of action is usually to follow through on the initial limits agreed upon by both parties.

The exception to this rule is a situation where the parishioner is facing some significant stress or crisis at the end of the five sessions and where there are no other available resources to provide the needed support. If this is the situation, an extension of a few sessions may be appropriate. However, this should again be time-limited and should take the form of crisis management. It should not involve more sessions than is absolutely necessary to restore some degree of stability to the parishioner's functioning or to introduce other people who can be of assistance.

Conclusion

Strategic Pastoral Counseling provides a framework for pastors who seek to counsel in a way that is congruent with the rest of their pastoral responsibilities and that is psychologically informed and responsible. While skill in implementing the model comes only over time, because the approach is focused and time-limited, it is quite possible for most pastors to acquire these skills. However, counseling skills cannot be adequately learned simply by reading books. As with all interpersonal skills, they must be learned through practice. Ideally, this practice is acquired in a context of supervisory feedback from a more experienced pastoral counselor.

The pastor who has mastered the skills of Strategic Pastoral Counseling is in a position to proclaim the Word of God in a highly personalized and relevant manner to people who are often desperate for help. This is a unique and richly rewarding opportunity. Rather than scattering seed in a broadcast manner across ground that is often stony and hard, even if at places it is also fertile and receptive to growth, the pastoral counselor has the opportunity to carefully plant one seed at a time. Knowing the soil conditions, he or she is also able to plant it in a highly individualized manner, taking pains to ensure that it will not be quickly blown away, and then gently watering and nourishing its growth. This is the unique opportunity for the ministry of Strategic Pastoral Counseling. It is my prayer that pastors will see the centrality of counseling to their call to ministry, will feel encouraged by the presence of an approach to pastoral counseling that lies within their skills and time availability, and will take up these responsibilities with renewed vigor and clarity of direction.

Introduction:
Counseling Worriers

The song swept the charts; all across America you could hear people humming the catchy little tune. Once it was embedded within the musical memory of the mind, it was there to stay. The song? "Don't Worry, Be Happy." Just reading the title will pop the tune into the minds of many. There was something about the thesis of the song that struck a common chord within us all. It said, "Here's a little song I wrote, learn to sing it note for note. Don't worry, be happy." That's what many of us are looking for: a less complex, simpler way of living. Truth is, that little jingle was a whole lot easier to sing than it ever was to live.

Worry is a funny thing. It has the ability to completely ignore social and spiritual boundaries. Poor people worry about getting money. Rich people worry about hanging onto it. The rich king Solomon once wrote, "Even at night my mind does not rest." Worry also ignores education and intellect. Fact is, educated people just worry more intelligently! Worry ignores age. Young people worry about finding the right mate, getting the right education, and landing the right job. Older people worry about running out of life before they run out of money. Middle-aged people are caught in the triple squeeze of worrying about the high cost of a college education for their children, caring for aging parents, and planning for their own retirement. Worry is one of the most common elements within our culture.

Worry in the Pastor's Personal Life

While most pastors would like to portray themselves as worry-free, many of us are fully aware of our clay feet. We know firsthand what it is to struggle with and worry about Sunday's message. Saturday nights are rarely very restful for the conscientious preacher. We all know that every audience contains some dear saints who disagree with our perspective and do not mind sharing their slant with us. We've all met those Monday morning quarterbacks out there who evaluate everything we do and say. For some bizarre reason, some people think that God has called them to be the Holy Spirit in our pastoral lives! No wonder we worry occasionally. In addition to that, the church's growth is often assumed to be our responsibility. If the church isn't growing or the offerings are down, there must be "something wrong." Then there are the committees. Who among us hasn't worried about a committee creating more pastoral problems than it solves? Add to all this the normal pressures of providing for our families financially, keeping our marriages exemplary, and maintaining control over our children. It's no wonder pastors worry.

Worrisome thoughts can be debilitating to us and our ministries. This summer I spent some time with a fellow pastor who was crippled by worry. The word translated "worry" in the New Testament is a combination of two words. One means "mind," the other means "divide." The concept is that worry has a dividing effect upon our minds. We become double-minded. James said that the double-minded person is unstable in all his ways. My pastor friend was clearly unstable. While he had pastored a very successful ministry for ten years, something went terribly wrong. He had watched it grow from a handful of new believers into a worship attendance well over a thousand. Without much warning, people began to grumble and second-guess his leadership. He endeavored to ride it out, but the criticism became unbearable. This gracious and godly human being, with a wonderful pastor's heart, was reduced to the shell of the man. As is often the case, the people closest to him had inflicted the deepest wounds. He was beaten up and broken.

Somewhere along the line he decided that it was best to leave the church. However, the damage went deep. He had lost his confidence and sense of direction. There are many pastors reading this who know the same gut-wrenching feeling. Now he is pastoring a new church. It's a good church, looking to my friend for leadership. However, he is paralyzed by the fear that something might go wrong again. He told me that he just could not give the direction and leadership necessary because he was worried that he might have a repeat performance of his previous church. He went on to say that another experience like that would kill him. He finds that the best he can do is be inactive or reactive. Pastors must be proactive, but the idea of being proactive carries too much risk. His worry has crippled him, and his ministry.

Every experienced pastor knows the precarious nature of our jobs. We've all had ministry friends who have crashed and burned due to little fault of their own. The pressure upon us to perform and the potential for failure certainly gives us plenty about which to worry. Given the worst case scenario, our thinking turns toxic. We experience an inner conflict that divides us emotionally, mentally, and spiritually. Our concern turns cancerous and begins to siphon the life and vitality from our hearts and minds. No wonder 57 percent of America's pastors believe that the church has "little positive impact on eternity or society." Many among us are crippled human beings, burdened by the weight of our eternal responsibility, as well as the real and perceived danger of daily ministry.

Most pastors reading this book will know what the Scriptures have to say concerning worry. Our hope is that as you read your heart will be ministered to as you endeavor to minister to others. Perhaps God will be able to restore faith, confidence, and a proactive mentality to some dear servants of Christ who are struggling with worrisome hearts.

Pastor's Attitudes toward Worriers

Our attitude as pastors is directed by Galatians 6:1: "Brothers, if someone is caught in a sin, you who are spiritual should restore him gently. But watch yourself, or you also may be tempted." God has given us the wonderful opportunity of gently restoring those who have been caught by a worrisome heart. The word picture within this verse is that of the medical world. The terminology described the setting of a broken bone or putting a joint back into place. Our attitude toward worriers should reflect the same kind of gentleness that we would expect from a doctor putting our shoulder back into joint.

Further, we should realize and admit that any of us, regardless of our maturity, are susceptible to worry. Even the most confident among us could fall prey to a worrisome heart given the wrong turn of events. Our attitude should be honest and nonjudgmental. Our counselees are not the enemy, they are victims of the enemy. They have come to us with their hearts in hand. Our task is not to condemn, but to comfort, instruct, and restore hope. We must view ourselves as people who have come alongside of fallen, fellow human beings and gently direct them back to the Scriptures and the Savior.

The Value of Ministry and Counseling of Worriers

According to the National Bureau of Standards, a dense fog covering seven city blocks to a depth of 100 feet is composed of less than one glass of water! That means that all the fog covering seven city blocks, it if were condensed together, could be held within a single drinking glass. Worry is like that. It clouds up reality. It chills us to the bone. It blocks the warmth and light of the sunshine. If we could see through the fog of worry and into the future, we would see our problems in their true light. Worry wouldn't blind us to reality, but instead our circumstances could be relegated to their true size and place. That's the goal of our five sessions together. If our counselees can reduce their worries to their actual and rightful size, they could probably stick them all into a water glass, too.

One study conducted on the subject of worry found that 40 percent of the things people worry about never happen. Another 30 percent of the things people worry about are things that can't be changed by worrying about them. An additional 12 percent turned out to be needless worry about health problems. Another 10 percent of peoples' worry centered around petty things like, "Did I turn off the lights?" "Is the dog fed?" "Will the store have what I'm looking for?" The study concluded that only 8 percent of the things people worry about could be considered "reasonable worry." Someone once said, "Worriers spend a lot of time shoveling smoke."

The value of counseling our people on the subject of worry rests upon two significant lines of reasoning. First, worry is common within our culture, and yet forbidden by the Scriptures. As pastors, our task is to communicate the truth of the Scriptures to a misdirected world. Second, as demonstrated in the previous paragraph, worriers waste huge amounts of time and emotional energy on what is generally a worthless activity. Strategic Pastoral Counseling of our people concerning worry can set them free to invest in the things of eternal value. Thus, the Word of God is honored by our people's obedience, they experience the blessing associated with conformity to the Scriptures, and ministry to our world is enhanced by emotionally and spiritually healthy people investing their lives in other people.

The Value of a Five-Session Format with Worriers

Strategic Pastoral Counseling is intended to be a brief and concentrated counseling experience. Background research conducted in the design of this model indicated that 87 percent of the pastoral counseling conducted by pastors generally involved five sessions or less. Given the time constraints of the typical pastor, this short-term model requires a concentrated focus with specific goals. Thus, we can make the maximum impact in the shortest time possible. The five-session process forces us to stay focused in our counseling, and communicates urgency to the counselee.

Use of the Client's Study Book

In addition to this text, we have designed a workbook to assist your client with homework assignments. It is a simple to follow, question and answer type of booklet. You will find that having your client use the workbook cuts down on your preparation time. It also directs your client's attention to the specific issues at hand and makes your sessions more profitable.

1

Worry Can Get You Down

The Psychology of Worry: An Overview

W e live in an age of anxiety. We should not be surprised then to see ourselves awash in worry, a chief indicator of anxiety. We are surrounded by worry. Christians worry; those outside the kingdom worry; all of us worry.

Worry, as far as we can know, is unique to the human race. Animals do not seem to spend time imagining what the future might bring and then fretting about it. Because we humans have the capacity to anticipate and to let our imaginations run wild, we are subject to OMIGOD thinking ("Oh, my God . . .").

The world around us gives us a lot about which we can worry. The future is very uncertain. Change is occurring at history's fastest pace. We cannot control the future. Our age breeds worry. And we are all affected.

Even the church seems better able to acknowledge the vulnerability of all of us to worry and anxiety. At one time we preferred to believe that Christians were never affected by these struggles. For example, John R. Rice could write in 1948, "Thank God, a Christian need never be unhappy, need never be defeated, need never be discouraged" (Rice 1948, 5). Very few Christian authors now claim that Christians are so removed from the problems of our age.

When our publishers were preparing to launch the Strategic Pastoral Counseling series, they conducted an extensive survey of pastors, asking for the most frequent problems their counselees brought to the counseling office. Worry and anxiety rated highly among the topics that Christian people frequently brought to their pastors (Benner 1992).

For many years psychologists did not give much attention to the concept of worry. Most researchers regarded it as a layperson's term, somewhat like "nervous breakdown," terms that did not merit serious definition. But in 1987 the term "worry" came of age when the latest diagnostic psychiatric manual listed worry as a primary symptom of the generalized anxiety disorder.

Anxiety has long been an important diagnostic category in the mental health field. Several years earlier the diagnostic procedure used with anxious patients was a process of elimination. First, the types of anxiety disorders that were very specific and focused would be eliminated: panic disorder, agoraphobia, obsessive-compulsive disorder, and post-traumatic stress disorder. Then all of the remaining anxious clients would be diagnosed as suffering from generalized anxiety disorder. In 1987, however, generalized anxiety disorder graduated from a residual category to a totally separate category mainly characterized by worry.

Now worry attracted the attention of researchers all over the world. With its new status as a primary symptom, science immediately got to work to learn about this long-neglected aspect of human misery. Study groups formed at major universities everywhere for the purpose of learning about worry. In the following sections of this chapter we have summarized the work to date of the research groups at Penn State, State University of New York at Albany, Louisiana State, and other places.

What Is Worry?

Because worry is so familiar to all of us, we can have trouble giving a precise definition to the troublesome habit. Our struggle is exactly the same struggle the experts face in distinguishing worry from anxiety, worry from fear, worry from panic, worry from concern, or worry from good, common-sense planning. The most common approach researchers now use is to define worry as the cognitive or thinking part of anxiety. Anxiety has additional physiological manifestations such as muscle tightness and a racing heartbeat. This approach to the definition of worry links the concept to anxiety; worry does not exhaust the meaning of anxiety, however, since other factors are present in that larger category of human struggles.

The experts disagree though when it comes to comparing worry to fear. Some theorists feel fear and anxiety/worry are close cousins with only minor differences. Other authors argue that fear/panic are totally distinct emotions. That particular debate is not germane to our task at hand, so we will leave that disagreement with them.

Dr. Thomas Borkovec, a researcher at Penn State who has earned the title of "Dr. Worry" because of his extensive study of the subject, has given us a helpful and complete definition of worry. He feels that "worry is a series of thoughts and images that are charged with negative emotion. These thoughts are relatively uncontrollable, and they concern some issue that has an uncertain outcome. The worrier is convinced, however, of the high probability that one or more negative outcomes will occur." If you have ever done extensive worrying yourself, you might compare your experience with the above definition to see if the definition fits.

The definition suggests several characteristics of worry. 1. Worry is oriented toward the future. When we worry, we are anticipating some dreaded event. Some people will say they worry a great deal about an event that happened in the past. But usually the substance of that worry concerns some future consequence of the past mistake or regretted occurrence. 2. Worry is a preoccupation of the self. Some worriers will talk about their worries with others, but the central feature of worry is that these troublesome thoughts are usually private and not vocalized. Aloneness is an apt descriptor for most worriers. 3. Another descriptive phrase to describe worry would be an anxious apprehension with some vigilance on the part of the worrier about an impending event. 4. Worriers have impaired habituation to stress. The more a "normal" person is exposed to stress the more the person adapts to it. But worriers seem to be equally jarred and troubled by stress every time they encounter a stressful situation; they do not habituate to it. 5. Finally, worriers vacillate among imagined, horrible outcomes with a tremendous lack of closure to the matter. Worriers often report an inability to know for certain just which dreadful outcome is most likely to occur.

Worriers catastrophize. That is, they are experts at imagining the worst of outcomes. Outsiders will often rate the objects of a worrier's concern as not very impressive; the worrier disagrees. When worriers describe what they fear will happen in the future, many of their concerns revolve around social themes. They fear ridicule, embarrassment, humiliation, or some other form of social disgrace. Worriers are very accomplished at spotting any kind of impending threat and then becoming greatly exercised over what that threat might mean to them.

Is some worry normal or is all worry bad for us? Some moderate levels of worry, and similarly some low levels of anxiety, probably help us rather than hinder us. For example, someone who is facing an examination will probably do better on the test with just a low level of anxiety to face the task. We usually change the terms though when we are talking about low levels of worry. We prefer to call good worry "concern," "constructive worry," "problem solving," or even "preparatory coping"! Most estimates of the frequency of worry suggest that about 15 percent of the population are chronic worriers, 30 percent are nonworriers, and the rest of us are somewhere in between.

How does worry compare to other mental illnesses? Many researchers are beginning to suggest that worry/anxiety and depression share a common substratum that makes them more similar to each other than we might otherwise think. Indications of this linkage come from the fact that antidepressant medications often have a very beneficial effect on anxious patients. Clinicians observe that all depressed clients are also anxious to some degree, but not all anxious clients are clinically depressed. Perhaps the best way to understand the possible connection between worry/anxiety and depression is to envision three gradations of distress. In the mildest form of worry, the client feels mild helplessness; in more pathological forms of worry (the types of people who will come to you for counseling), the client feels profound helplessness; but in depression the client has moved to strong feelings of hopelessness. In the two anxious or worrying stages, clients still are trying to cope; in depressive conditions they have given up hope.

The recent suggestion that anxiety/worry and depression are connected is prefigured in two characters in John Bunyan's *Pilgrim's Progress*. When Christian and his compatriots storm the great Doubting Castle and slay its master Giant Despair, they are then able to set free two imprisoned pilgrims: Mr. Despondency and his daughter Mrs. Much Afraid (Bunyan 1675). Perhaps these conditions ran in family lines, even 300 years ago!

In fact, research does suggest that people may inherit a vulnerability that affects whether they will become anxious worriers. Worry has other characteristics as well. Worry can eventually create health problems. Worry is complicated by the fact that it spirals; that is, as it continues it helps make itself worse. Worry is a self-feeding monster. Research has shown that worriers have narrowed attention. They tend to focus on stimuli that will trigger their worrying habit, namely signs of threat in the future. They do not notice or attend to other features of the environment. Good worriers will have many years of worry experience under their belts. Worry in its severe forms is most often chronic. Worry is so chronic, in fact, that some diagnosticians suggest we should consider worry as symptomatic of a personality disorder (an enduring maladaptive pattern of living) rather than as the main symptom of a transient disorder.

Finally, worry is a symptom of many psychiatric conditions in addition to generalized anxiety disorder. We can observe worry as a prominent symptom in various adjustment disorders, in the overanxious disorder, and in separation anxiety disorder.

Who Worries?

Chronic worriers are people who report worrying more than eight hours per day during the last six months. Nonworriers are people who do not describe themselves as worriers and who report worrying less than one-and-one-half hours per day. Even this level of worry is high and destructive. Worriers lack confidence, are irritable, and are often consumed in their gloomy reverie. Some research suggests that worriers are long sleepers. People of all ages

can be worriers, even children. Somewhat surprisingly, surveys
have indicated that young adults worry more than do senior adults.
Perhaps seniors worry less because they have less future about
which to worry. No one knows for sure.

What Do People Worry About?

People generally worry about events that fall into five categories:
1. Family/home/interpersonal matters; 2. Finances; 3. Work/school;
4. Illness/health/injury; 5. Routine daily activities and miscellaneous
matters. The content of a person's worry will vary depending on
the life circumstances of the person. The college student will tend
to worry about grades, examinations, and work placement after
graduation, whereas 60-year-old adults will tend to worry about
forced, early retirement, and whether pension planning has been
sufficient. Singles may worry about dating; married persons about
the future of their children.

Studies that have compared the worries of chronically anxious
people with the worries of "normals" have shown some interesting differences. The normal worriers are far more concerned with
finances and work/school issues than are chronic worriers. Chron-
ics, on the other hand, spend most of their worry time on ill-
ness/health/injury issues. Some research has suggested that when
the worrier is thinking about a future event that has a clearly preferred course of action, the worrier may be embroiled in even
greater indecision than when the issue is more ambiguous.

Another important study compared the worries of people in 1957
with the worries those very same people reported in 1976. Family
and personal issues predominated in 1957 whereas the same people were more concerned with finances and job security in 1976.

In summary, worriers can worry about anything that refers to
the self and that contains a hint of potential failure, shame, ridicule,
or personal embarrassment.

How Does Worry Work?

Researchers speculate that worriers selectively attend to threat
material. Worriers have an automatic processing bias toward envi-

ronmental threat. In other words, they have developed high sensitivities to future events that might pose some threat to their sense of self. They have an inflated sense of risk to the self. Secondly, worriers focus on the ambiguous features of that future event and attach negative consequences and outcomes to the ambiguity. Thirdly, the worrier assumes these threatening, future events are similar to painful events that have happened in the past. Most worry theories speculate that worriers have a highly developed and extensive catalog of past events that have indeed turned out in some disappointing manner. Fourthly, worriers then implement their highly developed skills of catastrophizing. They become consumed with "What if . . . " questions. The questions almost seem to drift automatically toward certain and impending incompetence that the future event will expose. Chronic worriers are very proficient at envisioning elaborate catastrophic scenarios, most of which have very low actual probabilities.

What Are the Consequences of Worry?

Worry has many consequences in the life of the chronic worrier, none of which are very positive. Even worriers themselves are often aware that the many hours they invest in the worrying process are not beneficial. Most worriers would like to stop the habit if they only knew how, partly because the worrier is painfully aware of the following consequences to their worry.

Worry Interferes with Performance

Poor performance in the context of excessive worrying is most clearly seen among people who worry about tests and examinations. Test anxiety is a crucial problem among college students, but agony over examinations can trouble people of all ages who are preparing for promotion examinations or other testing situations.

The worry begins long before the examination is scheduled. As the worrier frets about the upcoming exam and especially about the consequences of anticipated poor performance, vital time and energy is diverted from study and preparation for the test. Common sense tells us that performance is going to be poor when preparation for the testing procedure is inadequate. Worry continues to have a negative effect during the actual test itself. Worriers have trouble retrieving information that was learned, focusing on the specific instructions on the test, and providing a sample of their best effort. Worriers simply do more poorly on exams than non-worriers.

This poor-performance consequence of worry may be best seen in test anxiety but it is not limited to that task. Worrying about giving a speech, about constructing a playhouse, about drawing a picture, or about learning a language can result in similarly lowered performance levels.

Worry Produces Physiological Changes

While some studies have noted that worriers are long sleepers, as noted above, other research has shown that worry can also have the opposite result. Worry and insomnia are often connected. Worriers who have trouble falling asleep report that the bothersome and uncontrollable thoughts of worry that race through their minds as they are trying to sleep interfere with their ability to relax and to fall asleep.

Other physiological consequences are not so easily noticed by the worrier. Electroencephalogram (EEG) tests show brain wave differences when people are worrying. While brooding or attempting to solve problems, worriers have fewer of the brain waves that facilitate relaxation. Cortical activity increases especially in the left hemisphere. As a consequence, worriers are vigilant and uptight rather than relaxed.

In addition, worriers and the chronically anxious can often suffer from physical symptoms similar to those experienced by persons subject to acute stress: rapid palpitations, muscle tension, tremors, sweating, and gastrointestinal distress. These increased arousal rates, while true of people experiencing high levels of any of the major emotions, are detrimental to long-term health.

Worry Impairs Judgment

Worriers are known as people who make very poor subjective probability judgments. For example, on any given Sunday morning I face the task of driving five miles to church. The journey is rather routine and uncomplicated. In fact, I only make two turns on this particular trip. Normally I do not give this trip a second thought. I do not expect my car to break down on the way, nor do I worry much about the possibility of a flat tire. In fact, I pass several service stations along the way, even stations that are open early on Sunday mornings.

But if I were a good, experienced chronic worrier, I could spend large amounts of time in the hours before the scheduled departure time fretting over the possibility of car trouble on the way to church. I could just see myself stuck in the middle lane when a tire blows. What if I cannot get to the shoulder of the highway? What if someone did not put the car jack back properly last time it was used? What if I tear my clothes trying to change the tire? What if I am late, and they dismiss me as the Sunday school teacher? What if . . . ? What if . . . ? What if . . . ?

Nonworriers avoid the agony of this kind of worry by attaching very different levels of probability to all of these dreaded possibilities. Yes, a tire could blow out while in the middle of traffic but the probability is so low, I am not going to waste time worrying and fretting about it. Yes, the engine could stop running just when I am in the middle of a major intersection, but the likelihood of such a state of affairs is very low.

Why do worriers place high probabilities on events that actually have low probability? Perhaps because they have encoded in their memory banks past examples of dire happenings in such a vivid way that these stark and painful memories distort their vision of the future. The more worriers worry, the worse this problem of impaired judgment becomes.

Worry Fuels Anxiety

A final consequence of worry is its relationship to anxiety. Those who spend their lives studying anxiety are coming to the conclusion that ongoing worry maintains anxiety. Anxiety would normally dissipate in time unless some internal mechanism were keeping it active. Worry is the prime suspect in this situation. Clinicians are convinced that if we could help people turn off the almost automatic process of worry among chronic worriers, we could also control their anxiety states that often simply make their distress greater and more difficult to treat.

None of the above consequences of worry are very desirable outcomes. These distressing results give us all the more reason to want to help worriers contain and control their habit.

Why Do People Worry?

We have previously mentioned that worry is the cognitive side of anxiety. While we are anxious, worry is what is racing through our minds and somatic distress is what is happening to our bodies. Theories about the origins of worry thus have to consider the broader theories of how anxiety comes into being.

Theories of anxiety are many and sometimes very contradictory. Orthodox Freudian thought has always maintained that anxiety is a sign of internal conflict. Inside the psyche of an anxious person, according to psychoanalytic theory, wages a small war among various components of the person. The ego senses the impending emergence of an id impulse and immediately, with the help of the superego, prepares to make sure the impulse does not break forth.

The interpersonal psychiatry of Harry Stack Sullivan maintains that anxiety is a social phenomenon. In contrast to the Freudians who thought that anxiety was entirely internal, Sullivan argued that anxiety, and therefore worry, was the anticipation of failing to win the approval of some significant person in our life. Sullivan's theory corresponds closely to the finding that most worriers have a high level of social dread involved in their catastrophizing scenarios.

Some physiological theorists prefer to study anxiety without giving consideration to any underlying psychological correlates or causes. Their aim is to understand how the physiology of anxiety operates. Perhaps we will even discover some day, they assert, that the psychology of anxiety is merely the result of the physiology of anxiety.

Learning theorists have always maintained that we should understand anxiety primarily as a learned phenomenon. The learning of our anxiety is the result of reinforcement patterns. If we can identify these reinforcement schedules and alter them, we can help relieve people of their anxiety.

Cognitive theorists focus on the cognitions of worry. They point out that worriers, like many others who suffer from mental distress, entertain faulty ideas. These misbeliefs form the core of the worry process and must be changed before a person is ever free from its clutches.

A final school of theories regarding the nature and origins of anxiety is existentialism. Existentialists see anxiety as an identifying core of what it means to be human. Anxiety is not to be avoided but faced and resolved. Kierkegaard wrote that anxiety was the gap between "I might" and "I will," between my comprehension of a possibility and the choice I must make regarding that possibility.

Given the great variety of explanations offered by the above theories, we can feel overwhelmed when we face the question at hand: Why do people worry? Perhaps we can explore several possible answers to that question without having to make final decisions among the many theories listed above. The most prominent answers to this question suggested by current research follow.

Because They Dread a Loss of Control

We have already seen that worry for the chronic sufferer is relatively uncontrollable. The pressured thoughts seem to come even when the worrier has determined to ban them or never to indulge in them again. But controllability plays yet another important role in worry.

Worriers may be convinced that in order to be prepared for the future, to avoid being caught by surprise, and to minimize the risk of the future, they must try to anticipate every possible eventuality that could occur. Thus when and if some terrible event does actually happen, the occurrence will not take them by surprise and therefore they will be more in control of the situation. Perhaps such "logic" predominates early in the worrier's career. Later the pattern of excessive and morbid preoccupation with impending failure takes on a life of its own and perpetuates itself.

Researchers often call this aspect of worry the "illusion of control," since worrying does not actually increase the amount of control a person will have over the future. A corollary to this initial attempt to control can be the fear that if I do not worry, negative outcomes are more likely to occur. This type of magical thinking can operate powerfully even though the worrier might be able to admit to an interviewer that such "logic" does not make much sense at all.

As with many other psychological conditions, the reason for the inception of a problem may not always explain why the pattern continues. In this case, efforts to gain control may help understand how people begin their careers as worriers. But then we may have to resort to other explanations for its continuance. In one major study, worriers rated their worries at about a 75 point stress level (on a scale of 100, with 100 being absolutely catastrophic). But when asked to estimate what their stress level would be should their dreaded fears come true, they rated them at a 50–60 point stress level. In other words, the worry process had taken on a life of its own and they were captive to it.

If an effort to control truly does help explain why people worry, we can make one additional speculation that might help us as we counsel worriers. Worriers may have in their backgrounds some painful experiences with uncontrollability. These past events may stand out in the person's memory and may have a significant shaping role to play in the person's current life.

An example of this factor comes from a short autobiographical story written by Stanley Bing. Bing was called into his boss's office to explain why Bing had done such a poor job writing an important report. As Bing was climbing the stairs toward the office of his boss, his mind tortured him with an almost endless cascade of "What if . . . ?" questions. What if the boss fires me? How can I tell my wife? What if she doesn't understand and leaves me? How will I survive? On and on the questions raced through his mind as he approached the office. In those few moments he did what all good worriers do: got lost in imagined dismal outcomes to the matter at hand.

Bing paused before facing the boss. Soon his mind was flooded with a memory.

> When I was eight, I went to visit my grandfather in the city. If you think I'm a jolly fellow now, you should have seen me then; I was

positively jejune. It was May, I remember, and the world was as big and wide and hopeful as the first day of summer vacation. I rang the bell. There was no answer. I could hear the TV blaring inane laughter beyond the door, and I thought, "Come on, Stan, there's twenty-six potential explanations for this phenomenon. Why assume the worst?" An hour later, my mother joined me with the key and we entered that apartment. My grandfather was lying on the living-room floor. He was alive, but he looked tiny, diminished. . . . The man was with us for five or six years after that, and we relished every one, but an ultimate reality had reasserted itself with a vengeance, and for good (Bing 1989, 101).

Bing then may share with other worriers a background that includes some shocking or shameful or overpowering experience that any sane person would want to avoid ever happening again. Hence the need to control by worry. We will later see that counselors can look for this possible background in their worried counselees. Sometimes knowing why we dread the future so much can help us quiet our worry mechanisms.

Because They Are Avoiding Other Issues

Another more complicated explanation for why people worry also emerges from current research. Psychologists have suggested that people worry so as to avoid other, more painful experiences. For example, researchers have noticed that when people are instructed to worry, no measurable autonomic system changes seem to occur. Their blood pressure does not seem to rise, no change occurs in heart rate, and muscles do not tense up. EEG results can detect brain wave changes, but autonomic changes do not appear. Some worry experts speculate that worry, because it is such a verbal, linguistic activity, prevents the arousal of images in the mind. Images, or imaginal thinking, is much more highly linked to the somatic components of anxiety. Thus worriers may have discovered that by worrying they can avoid an even worse experience, the somatic or affective components of anxiety.

If such an explanation is correct, we can understand better why worriers have such a struggle giving up the habit. If their worry is serving a secondary purpose, namely helping them avoid the feelings or somatic sensations associated with anxiety, then they have a "good" reason not to give up their patterns of worry. This possibility will help us when we get to session two with our worrying clients. Helping them face their anxiety rather than avoid the anxiety will facilitate their ability to change.

Because They Possess Immature Problem-Solving Skills

Observers have pointed out that our worry process is actually a conversation with ourselves. Persons who solve problems with dispatch and ease also have these conversations with themselves. But the content is vastly different. The nonworrier is also aware of impending events or activities. "I know that job promotion interview is coming up on Wednesday next week. I want to make sure I get a good night of rest Tuesday. I think I'll wear my new blue suit. If I don't make it this year, I'll just try again next time." The nonworrier approaches the stressful event with good problem-solving skills. Fully aware of both personal strengths and weaknesses, the nonworrier focuses on action and what he or she can do ahead of time to be best prepared.

The worrier often does not have such effective problem-solving skills. Instead of being able to define the problem, identify action options, and perform these actions, the worrier is stuck on step one: endlessly identifying eventualities and possibilities. Few, if any, plans for action come to mind.

Worrying of this kind has a prototype in the young child who is worried about an upcoming trip to the zoo. The child asks mother, "What if grandma comes while we are gone to see the monkeys?" A helpful mother will answer, "She'll just wait for us to come home." The child expresses an honest question and receives a satisfactory answer. Worriers ask the same kind of honest questions, multitudes of them in fact, but they never seem to receive within themselves any satisfactory answers. Worriers behave as if they have never internalized a patient parental voice that could answer terrifying questions with peaceful, calming answers.

In summary, worriers may have immature problem-solving skills. They may lack the ability to get beyond the problem-defining stage that nonworriers take so much for granted. Again, this reason for worrying may help identify for us some useful interventions when we get into our counseling process with worriers.

Perhaps none of the above suggestions regarding why people worry is totally satisfactory. Maybe some combination of these factors will best explain the worry patterns of our worried counselees. We must move on to the last relevant question of our overview.

What Helps Worriers?

In this book we are taking a Christian approach to the treatment of worry. Many of the biblical strategies for controlling and/or eliminating worry from our lives do not emerge from psychological research on the subject. However, we will find that many of the proven strategies for effective treatment of worry are, in fact, consistent with the Bible. Certainly we must add to the approaches suggested by the scientific literature those interventions that the Bible suggests. In so doing we will have an even more powerful set of helping tools when we work with worriers. First, though, we need to survey the approaches suggested by current research as most effective in curbing worry patterns.

Some basic factors can greatly help worriers. They must see that the problem needing change resides inside themselves. Few worriers will attempt to blame others for their struggles with worry, but counselors can remind worriers of this basic fact nonetheless. Worriers need to realize that they can change, that they can control if not conquer worry with God's help, and that they also have the power to change some features of their environments that foster their struggles with worry.

The following list of interventions represents some of the most effective treatments therapists currently use with worriers. The categories below have a great deal of overlap. They are not all mutually exclusive; therapists can use a combination of these approaches. Some treatments have been tested on a particular form of worry with the hope that they will also be effective with other types of worry.

Skills Training

Therapists working with college students who experience high levels of test anxiety have obtained excellent results with skills training. The theory behind this approach is that the students do not have some needed skills that would ordinarily help them curb the tendency to worry about the test. The skills that the therapists taught these students included: 1. Early detection of anxiety signals. Thus students would learn to monitor anxiety signals early in the worry process so that the students could intervene before the worry process consumed them. 2. Environmental self-management. Students learned how to identify factors in their environment that elevated their worry and how to change those factors. 3. Relaxation. We will discuss this skill later in this section; relaxation is a part of many effective treatment strategies with worriers. 4. Cognitive control. Students identified parts of their self-talk that were setting them up for failure. They learned easy steps for controlling these thoughts and thus approached their test with a better frame of mind.

In another application of skills training, some researchers sent worried students home with a manual. The therapists briefly showed the students how to self-administer the manual's program for skill acquisition. Otherwise the therapists did not meet with the students. These students did show improvement in how they managed upcoming tests, but students who had learned the new skills under the tutelage of a therapist did even better. Apparently the mentoring aspect of counseling is a helpful part of the process.

The main advantage of skills training is its simplicity. Worriers can easily learn all the components of the training. The power of the method probably stems from the combination of skills that the therapist teaches.

Problem Solving

The problem-solving approach to help worriers shares many features with the skills acquisition method. The problem-solving method is structured, goal-oriented, focused on change in the here and now, designed to remove blame from the worrier, and geared to instill optimism. The aim of the method is to increase the client's ability to deal with problems in general, not just the immediate issue.

The problem-solving method is well-known to all of us: Identify the problem, list solutions to the problem, choose which course of action to take, implement the chosen solution. Worriers, as we have discussed earlier, are experts in step one. But they never seem to progress beyond the listing of possibilities, mostly negative ones of course. Problem-solving training helps them get beyond this impasse.

An Australian researcher has suggested that worriers suffer from a coping strategy mismatch. Worriers try to tackle uncontrollable life events. Research shows that the preferred problem-solving strategy for dealing with such major events is a problem-solving method that includes dealing with the emotions generated by the issue. Worriers are so focused on the cognitive ingredients of their struggle, however, that they often overlook dealing with the affective side of the problem. Hence they are trying to problem solve with the wrong problem-solving method. As we shall see later, helping worriers deal with their feelings is an important part of effective helping.

Stimulus Control

Stimulus control is a technical name for a very simple strategy. Therapists instruct worriers to identify a 30-minute period in the day that can be dedicated to worry and to nothing else. The ideal time for the worry period is late afternoon. Thus the worrier will have time to collect worries during earlier parts of the day that will make up the agenda for the 30-minute worry session, and the worry period will not be late enough in the day so as to interfere with sleep. Worriers keep a notebook of worries that pop into their minds during the day. Then they are instructed to postpone thinking about the worries until they can return to their list during the worry period. Therapists help worriers make constructive use of these 30 worry minutes by processing the worries in a problem-solving mode. If the 30 minutes eventually seems too long to worriers, they must force themselves to worry for the full 30 minutes. After four weeks worry levels should significantly decrease.

Research has shown that the full 30-minute time frame is an important factor in making this technique work. Studies have proven that a 15-minute worry period can have the opposite effect by making the client's worrying worse. A full 30 minutes, for some reason, appears to be necessary for success.

Cognitive-Behavioral Treatment

Cognitive-behavioral treatment is a well-known approach to psychotherapy. Studies have shown that this approach works well with worriers because the method attacks two central features of the worriers' predicament: their captivity to destructive thinking (cognitive) and their inability to take action (behavioral). In fact, either approach by itself (cognitive or behavioral) has a markedly lesser chance to help worriers significantly.

We will later explore the patterns of destructive thinking that beset worriers. Their catastrophizing tendencies provide them with many worst-case scenarios that consume their thought patterns. The cognitive sections of this treatment regimen seek to elucidate these destructive qualities of the worrier's thinking so that more constructive thoughts can be substituted.

Worriers are also well-known for their inability to act or to take constructive actions that would free them from their endless worries. The behavioral aspects of this treatment regimen attack this avoidance behavior.

Cognitive-behavioral treatment seeks to give the worrier a great sense of self-control and independence. The treatment is highly structured and aims at giving clients explanations about how their worry patterns have developed and why they are destructive. The treatment also gives clients a blueprint that helps explain what has helped them during the course of therapy and how these factors can help them on an ongoing basis.

Medication

Occasionally an anxious worrier will be more interested in taking a pill to get rid of the bothersome worry patterns than engaging in some hard work therapy. Medication can be helpful in treating anxious people. Several years ago a new class of minor tranquilizers (benzodiazepines) enjoyed great success in treating anxiety. Only later did we become familiar with some of the problems associated with long-term use of these drugs. Newer medications (azapirones) currently seem to have value in helping people deal with their anxiety.

As we mentioned earlier in this survey, tricyclic medications, normally used to fight depression, have been effective with many anxious patients. Physicians do not know the exact reason for this effective response to the medicine. These medications are generally safer than the minor tranquilizers so their effectiveness may be a hopeful treatment for some worriers.

Counselors who feel a worrier could benefit from medication will, of course, have to refer the counselee to a physician. In no case, however, will medicine by itself be sufficient to help a worrier conquer worry. Other counseling will be necessary to accomplish that goal.

Relaxation

The final treatment we will discuss is relaxation. Recently many Christian critics of counseling have questioned the use of relaxation training. They fear that relaxation will introduce some anti-Christian influences into the believer's life. However, relaxation is not a magical, mysterious, questionable technique. Relaxation is simply a purposed calming of one's life so that the client can be more in control. Relaxation is the opposite of being uptight, a condition that is surely not a Christian virtue.

Relaxation, especially when coupled with one of the other treatments listed above, is a proven help to worriers. Their worry patterns have kept them in a vigilant frame of mind that eventually lowers their abilities to function well. Progressive relaxation techniques, not mantra-induced relaxation, lowers cortical activity in the brain's left hemisphere. Relaxation and worry appear to be unfriendly to one another. If I worry, I am not relaxed; if I am relaxed, I am going to have trouble worrying.

This survey of effective treatments gives us many ideas for useful approaches to helping the worriers who come to our office for counseling. We will now look at a five-session model for working with these people in great need of our help.

2

Don't Worry about It

The Encounter Stage: Session 1

The Bible and Worry

Let's begin with the issue of faith. Everyone lives every day by faith. By faith you drive your car, trusting your very existence to a couple of rubber hoses filled with brake fluid. Every time you eat out, you do so by faith in the cook and the server. When you climb aboard an airplane, you place your faith in a whole host of engineers, maintenance personnel, the control tower, and flight crew. Every time you turn on the faucet to get a drink of water, you do so by faith. You place your health in a filter system that you've never seen! Faith is not an optional activity for twentieth-century people. The only real option is the object of our faith, and it is the object of our faith that determines whether or not we will struggle with worry.

We begin this chapter with a discussion of faith, because faith is the exact opposite of worry. Most of us don't worry about the tap water because we have learned through past experience that it's okay to drink. We never give a second thought to applying pressure to the brake peddle because it has always stopped us in the past.

We simply have no good reason to believe that the brakes will not stop us again. The point is: we *learn* to live by faith. Learning to live by faith is the first biblical step toward eliminating worry from our lives.

Faith is so crucial to our spirits that Hebrews 11:6 identified it as an absolute if we hope to please God. "And without faith it is impossible to please God, because anyone who comes to him must believe that he exists and that he rewards those who earnestly seek him." Faith is the oil in the machinery of life; worry is the sand. A little sand can go a long way toward destroying expensive equipment. Likewise, a little worry can grind away at your confidence for living and leave you paralyzed.

Faith is not some magical whammy that comes upon us suddenly. Faith is learned. The first step of that learning process is to admit to ourselves that we really do live every day by faith. Once that is understood, it's not far to the next step of realizing that if you are willing to trust a cook or pilot whom you do not know and who is capable of making a mistake, why not learn to trust the God you do know who never makes an error? Having admitted that faith in God is necessary, next we need to turn to the source of faith building. Clearly, the best source for personal faith enhancement is the Bible. Romans 10:17 states: "Consequently, faith comes from hearing the message, and the message is heard through the word of Christ." The word of Christ is the Bible. As you begin to read and internalize Scripture, faith in the author begins to grow. Since faith is the exact opposite of worry, worry will begin to evaporate.

Understanding the role of faith is the positive side of the equation. Identifying worry for what it really is, is the other. Like it or not, worry is wrong. Unless one is willing to admit this, justification and rationalization will continue to grant worry a foothold in your heart. Jesus said, "Therefore do not worry about tomorrow, for tomorrow will worry about itself. Each day has enough trouble of its own" (Matt. 6:34). The phrase *"Do not worry,"* is not a divine suggestion. Jesus was not sheepishly implying that "worry was a bad idea." He gave a direct emphatic command that, when violated, equals sin. Jesus labeled worry for what it is: sin. He stated that his followers were not to worry about tomorrow and suggested an alternative. The alternative was to let tomorrow worry about tomorrow. As ironic as it may sound, Jesus was forcing his followers to focus upon today. He was not willing to concede even the slightest concession in the arena of worry about the future. Since human beings do not worry about the past, Jesus did not leave us much about which to worry! Some may argue that they worry about the past; but the truth is, they are worrying about the future ramifications of the past, and that is therefore off-limits by divine decree.

We think there are several reasons why Jesus said what he did about worry. First of all, worry accuses God of being a liar. God has promised to meet all of your needs (Phil. 4:19). Needs are one of the things we worry about. Worry blatantly disagrees and argues that God is either unable or unwilling to fulfill that promise in your life. Second, worry questions the sovereignty of God. He has promised to use everything that comes into our lives for good (Rom. 8:28). God is never caught by surprise. Worry finds a thousand reasons why God's promise cannot possibly be true under the current circumstances. Further, worry questions the sincerity of God. God has promised that he will never abandon you. In Hebrews 13:5–6 God states: "Never will I leave you; never will I forsake you." Worry erodes away our faith, and causes us to wonder if God will really be there when we need him. Apparently, the confidence of God's presence was enough for the writer of Hebrews, since he went on to say, "So we say with confidence, 'The Lord is my helper; I will not be afraid. What can man do to me?'"

Worry denies and ignores all of these promises. It plays the "yeah-but" game: "Yeah but, what if the doctor finds something wrong?" "Yeah but, you don't know my husband." "Yeah but, there are times when the Lord has not come through for me the way he should." The "yeah-buts" of life are endless. The problem is, worry knows them all and enjoys playing the game. The "yeah-buts" of worry force your eyes off of God and onto something that might or might not happen. Suddenly, you are living in the world of fantasy and fear. Whether your fears become reality or not is irrelevant to the game. Once the focus is off of God, your potential problems (underscore the word "potential") will loom larger than life.

Finally, worry questions the personal nature of God. The prophet Isaiah offered some wonderful words of reassurance. "So do not fear, for I am with you; do not be dismayed, for I am your God. I will strengthen you and help you; I will uphold you with my right-eous right hand" (Isa. 41:10). Worry is unwilling to admit that the God of the Universe cares enough to make those words a reality for you. The verse contains some very direct commands and equally direct promises. It charges us, *"Do not fear."* Worry is little more than fear. Worry is the fear of what might happen. It is also the fear of what might not happen. God had a very logical reason for his command; he said, *"For I am with you."* Can you think of a better reason to lay aside fear? If the eternal God, creator of the universe, sustainer of all life, omnipotent, omniscient, and omnipresent says, "I'm with you," why are you worried? Would God lie to you? When worry begins to play the "yeah-but" game, your best response is "yeah-but, God is with me."

It also says, *"Do not be dismayed."* The word dismayed is from a primary root that means "to gaze." It was used to describe one who looked in amazement or bewilderment. It carried the idea of being paralyzed, unsure of any course of action. It is a feeling of helplessness. It is how you feel when your world is out of control. God says that we need not be dismayed because *"I am your God."* Here the promise offered to us rests squarely upon his personal relationship with us. As *your* God, he is on call every moment of every day. He never takes a nap, he never goes on vacation.

Following the two commands, God made three very practical promises. First, he said, *"I will strengthen you."* The word for strengthen means "to be alert" or "to be fortified with courage." Putting those thoughts together, it means that God will enable you to be alert to your circumstances and grant you whatever courage is necessary to cope with them. Second, God promised to *"help you."* The word used for help meant "to surround." The concept is simply beautiful. Picture yourself surrounded by the loving hands of the almighty God. That makes you bulletproof. Nothing can touch you without his knowledge and his permission. Finally, God offered these words: *"I will uphold you."* The word translated uphold means to "sustain." That's a great conclusion to a fabulous promise. It was God's way of saying he will sustain, surround, and strengthen you for as long as necessary!

Getting Started

Laying the right foundation is crucial to redirecting the thoughts and feelings of counselees. The foundation you'll want to establish is twofold. First, you need to portray yourself as one who is willing to listen well without condemning. During this first session you'll be laying some pretty direct information on your client. That is why you must be a gracious listener and gentle counselor. You really need to put aside the "preacher" role and cultivate the role of "comforter." Most of you reading this will quickly recognize the difference between the two. One is concerned with proclaiming truth through directness and conviction. The other technique is equally concerned with truth but endeavors to deliver it through a gentle persuasion. Hebrew 10:24–25 describes it well. "And let us consider how we may spur one another on toward love and good deeds. Let us not give up meeting together, as some are in the habit of doing, but let us encourage one another—and all the more as you see the Day approaching." The word translated "consider" is an intensified form of "to think." It means that we are to carefully observe and contemplate how we might be able to "spur" them along. The word for "spur" was used to describe the gentle and repetitive process of sharpening a knife. Just as knife sharpening is a slow but effective process, we are to patiently and repeatedly expose them to truth. Little by little, they will begin to experience subtle changes. With each change will come the encouragement to keep going. This verse is a reminder that you'll need to listen for the feelings behind the words and respond to where the person is, rather than where you would like them to be. Hebrews 10 states that the net result of this style will be the encouragement of our clients. Even the word "encourage" graphically describes our role. It is the same word used in the New Testament to describe the person and work of the Holy Spirit. God has called us into a partnership with him where we approach people from the outside with the same gentle directness that his Spirit approaches them from the inside. When we adopt that kind of mind-set, we naturally cultivate an environment where we can deliver truth without offending or condemning our brothers and sisters.

The second objective of this first session is to help the client understand and accept the Bible's basic perspective on worry. The goal, at this point, is to acquaint your client with concepts mentioned earlier in the chapter. You will want to help them to understand that all of us live every day by faith. Some may protest that concept, but as you illustrate it to them they will begin to get the picture. Next, you'll want to direct their thoughts toward the objects of their faith. Help them see the humorous inconsistency between trusting strangers (like the guy that works on your car) with a hesitancy to trust God. You'll need to cultivate the notion that faith is the opposite of worry. Help them understand that worry and faith are mutually exclusive concepts which, by nature, oppose one another. Have them articulate the idea that "faith is the oil in the machinery of life, worry is the sand."

Once they understand the role of faith, you'll want to move them into the Bible's commentary on worry. Let them read aloud the verses we used earlier in the chapter. What's important at this point is simply to expose them to the word of God. We are not asking or expecting them to read a verse on worry and respond with a naive, "Oh, well then, I'm okay now." We are not asking them to "own" the truth of the Scriptures. Rather, the hope is that your client will be willing to admit objectively that the Scriptures about worry are true and that they represent a desirable objective. In many respects, the biblical foundation that you will lay during this first session, will become the ultimate goal of your counseling together. The hope is that by your final meeting together, they will have been able to internalize and embrace the biblical exhortations concerning worry. They must understand that the purpose of your sessions is primarily real life change, not emotional hand-holding.

Second Corinthians 10:5 is an excellent summary of what you intend to accomplish. You should have your client read it aloud. "We demolish arguments and every pretension that sets itself up against the knowledge of God, and we take captive every thought to make it obedient to Christ." The goal is to provide them with the tools necessary to demolish all the arguments of the "yeah-but" game. The purpose is to enable them to take captive every thought of worry and bring their lives into the obedience of Christ, who stated categorically, "Do not worry." As they understand the goal, and become willing to aggressively pursue it, real change will occur.

Taking a Worry History

An important task in the first session for you as a counselor is to take a history of your counselee's experience with worry. Your client may be a parishioner whom you know quite well. But your new counseling relationship with that person requires that you know additional information—in this case, about this person's worry patterns.

You may already know basic demographic information about this person: age, occupation, marital and family history, church affiliation, and experience with Christianity. If you do not know this basic information about the person, you should obtain this data during the first session.

You will also need to know, in the client's own words, just exactly what is the content of his or her current worries. If the client responds with a vague, "I guess I just worry about everything," you will want to press for some specific and recent examples. Remember that our definition of worry involves forms exaggerated and improbable expectations built around future events that are not likely to be so negative in their actuality. By urging your client to specify worry content, you will be verifying that this person does indeed suffer from undue worry.

Occasionally you might encounter people who describe themselves as worriers when in fact they are not. For example, a person may be facing some objective future events that in most everyone's view could well be catastrophic. In this case the counselee might need our pastoral care in preparing for the unknown, but we might not deal with them in the same way we would with someone whose dread regarding the future is obviously exaggerated.

Next you will want to know some history of these and similar worries. How long has the counselee been worrying in this way? What are examples of other worries the counselee can recall struggling with? How many of the dreaded outcomes have actually come true?

Next, attempt to discover how widely the counselee has shared this tendency to worry. If the counselee has shared this inner struggle with a spouse or some other person closely related, what has been the response given to the counselee? Have family members tried to be understanding?

Does the counselee know of other family members who also worry? Did the counselee's parents worry? If so, how did the children know about it? Does the counselee recall worrying as a child? What about?

If you will be using the book *Why Worry?*, you will notice that one of the questions your counselee will answer is, "Can you recall events from your childhood when you felt deeply embarrassed or humiliated?" We will use the answer to this question in a subsequent counseling session. But we should not pose the question directly in this first counseling session since the material may be too intrusive for our first conversation. Posing the question in the client handbook will also have the advantage of giving the counselee some time to ferret out an answer from long-term memory.

Finally, you as a counselor will want to obtain some understanding about what the counselee has already done in an attempt to stop worrying. Has the counselee ever had any other professional help for the problem? Has the counselee tried to self-correct for this struggle? If so, how and with what success?

When you know all the above information about the worrier sitting in front of you as a counselee, you will be better prepared to make plans for the following four sessions. The information you gather from your worry history may also help you gauge how closely your client fits the normal patterns of worriers.

First-Session Jitters

The first counseling session can be somewhat nerve-wracking for the worrier and for the counselor. If you as a pastoral counselor have extensive experience, the first session may not wrack your nerves at all. But your counselee may not be so calm about the matter. In fact, this counseling session may be the counselee's first-ever counseling experience.

Any good worrier, we must remember, will possess finely perfected skills of fretting over future events. We can be sure that your new counselee has worried about this first session. Because we know that worriers can anticipate the most nonthreatening event and imagine the worst from it, we can be sure that they have viewed this first session in precisely this way.

A main task of the counselor is to set the counselee at ease about the entire process. As a pastor you should be able to accomplish this task well, even though some worriers can resist our reassuring statements.

In addition to these generic tasks for the counselor, worriers present some unique challenges to the pastoral counselor that we will briefly discuss.

Issues of control may well surface in working with the worrier. A major question, "Who is in charge here?" will not surface verbally during the session, but the issue may be just below the surface. Some people who have developed patterns of chronic worry have also used their worry to control others. This secondary purpose to their worry can present a clear challenge to the counselor who tries to arrange for a brief series of five counseling sessions. If your worrying friends resist your suggestions regarding the planned number of sessions, about the goals you want them to adopt for their counseling, or about the homework they need to do during this process, you may have encountered the issue of control. Gently, firmly, and clearly you must assert your leadership of the process. Eventually your planning and structure of the process will prove reassuring even to the most controlling of worriers.

Some counselees fit into the counseling process with great ease: they talk just enough, they listen just enough. Occasionally, however, you encounter a counselee who simply will not talk much at all. Information is hard to obtain, statements are brief and minimal, and the counselor feels compelled to do most of the talking during the session. Your best response to this type of client is to continue building rapport, to repeat your initial statements that the counseling process works best when the counselee can talk and share honestly, and to show appreciation when the counselee does talk freely with you.

An opposite problem arises when a counselee dominates the session by talking incessantly. In this instance the counselor feels frustrated in trying to accomplish the goals of the session such as taking the worry history. Again the counselor may need to assert some control here by making sure that your questions are specific and that the counselee knows the counseling session must be interactive, not a one-way street.

The counselor must remember that three certainties will apply to every worrier who comes for counseling. First, worriers will already know that they worry and that they worry excessively. Chronic worriers have heard this feedback from many other people during their lives. They do not need you to be the next one in a long line of people who have said, in effect, "You worry too much." What worriers need from you as a pastoral counselor is a word of hope. Hope that in spite of their struggles with worry, they can change. Hope that with some planning and commitment this counseling process will help them control their problem. Worriers do not need counselors to dump heavy judgmental comments on them such as, "Well you know that you are sinning and grieving the Holy Spirit by worrying when the Bible has clearly told you not to."

Second, other people have tried to help your counselee with the worry problem. Perhaps a spouse has shared, "You just need to . . . " with the worrier. Friends may have shared how they have successfully conquered worry. Sometimes the endless number of stories about how worry is not that hard to control from people trying to be helpful have accomplished nothing more than to heap discouragement onto your client. Again, the best strategy for you as a counselor is to reassure the worriers that your role is not simply to tell them how to conquer the problem; your role is to work alongside them and to be for them a helper, not just an advisor.

Third, we can also be certain that the worriers who come to you for help have probably already tried to self-correct for the problem and have failed. The most frequent affect counselees bring to the counseling office is one of discouragement. Again, a fresh and vital investment you can make in the lives of these downhearted worriers is to extend to them some hope. In Christ they can experience freedom from the oppressive weight of their worry.

Use of Scripture and Prayer

The hope you instill within your client must extend beyond your office. They need to have the tools necessary to combat those helpless and hopeless feelings that will come their way. Prayer and the Scriptures will play a vital role in this process.

For most people, the Bible is a confusing and difficult book to understand. As a pastor, you have made a living by making it your business to understand the Bible. You have gone to college or seminary and received hundreds of hours in specialized training to help you understand this ancient document. That makes it easy for the professional to forget just how foreign the Bible really is to our people. Furthermore, our culture is becoming increasingly secular in its thinking and training. The average guy in the street or in the boardroom has virtually no understanding of what used to be common biblical knowledge. That is why people tend to shy away from reading the Bible on their own. It takes time, and it is foreign turf anyway. This has left a generation biblically illiterate. For example, a recent Gallup poll revealed that 60 percent of Americans did not know what "the Holy Trinity" was. Sixty-six percent couldn't identify who delivered the Sermon on the Mount, and 79 percent were unable to name a single Old Testament prophet. The truth is, most people have never sat down to read the Bible. We need to help them with this.

Our purpose, at this point, is to help them appreciate the priceless value of the word of God. Our hope is that they will become willing to make a daily investment in themselves by investing a few minutes in daily Bible reading.

Your client probably will not know where to begin. You certainly do not want them randomly picking passages that have no relevance to the issue at hand. We recommend that the worrier read the passages on the next page for the seven days before the next counseling session. Each of them focuses upon the ability of Jesus to provide for people's needs.

You will want them to go beyond just blasting through the verses to keep you off their back. The hope is that they will begin to form a habit as they see the value of biblical input. I've found that the

Day 1: Matthew 6:24–34	Jesus' Advice on Worry
Day 2: Matthew 8:5–17	The Faith of the Centurion
Day 3: Matthew 13:1–9, 18–22	The Parable of the Sower
Day 4: Matthew 14:14–33	Feeding 5000 and Walking on the Water
Day 5: John 5:1–14	Healing at the Pool of Bethesda
Day 6: John 10:1–18	Jesus as the Good Shepherd
Day 7: John 14:1–14	Jesus Comforts his Disciples

easiest way for people to get beyond a superficial reading is to have them look for the answers to the five following questions.

1. Is there a sin to confess?
2. Is there a promise to claim?
3. Is there an action to avoid?
4. Is there a command to obey?
5. Is there an example to follow?

These five questions can be applied to nearly every passage of Scripture and help the reader develop the ability to read for life application. While every passage won't contain answers for every question, every passage does answer at least one of them and helps direct the reader's attention to the main purpose of the text. Answering these questions, and jotting down some thoughts about each, can be the beginning of a daily time with the word for your client. Assure them that it should take no more that 15 minutes and will be well worth the investment!

In addition to reading the Scriptures, encourage them to develop a prayer journal that focuses upon the issue of worry. Sometime before they retire for the evening, have them reflect back on the day and make a complete list of the things that worried them. That list will become their prayer list for the duration of your counseling sessions. When they worry about something new they should add it to the list. Each night they should pray about the items on the list. By doing so they will be fulfilling the biblical directive of Philippians 4:6, which is a major step toward removing worry. While they may continue to worry about the issues on the list, they will be moving in the right direction. During the weeks ahead, some, if not most, of the things they have worried about will come to some conclusion. As they do, you will want them to find the specific area of worry on their list and write next to it what happened in response to their prayers. During the course of your sessions together they will (with your help) begin to see that many of the events they worried about never actually happened. Seeing that on paper will really help counter future worries. Further, they will notice that God gave them the grace and strength to handle what life has brought their way.

Getting Ready for Session Two

Why Worry? is a small booklet designed to accompany this book. The counseling approach we are describing here does not require that you use the booklet with your counselee, but you may find that having your counselee work through the booklet will strengthen the counseling process. Worriers can also use the *Strategic Christian Living* series on their own without necessarily being in counseling for the problem.

The five chapters in the booklet correspond with the five sessions you will hold with your worrier. We find that the accompanying title is most effective when the counselee reads chapter one after the first session and so forth, although some other pattern of use may work just as well for you.

Each chapter in *Why Worry?* will involve worriers in answering questions and recording specific information about their worry. This study format serves our counseling purposes well because it involves counselees in action, a needed ingredient in their efforts to conquer worry.

At the end of session one, you will need to review briefly the five session format, your expectations for the counselee between each of these five sessions, and specifically how to prepare for session two. You will notice that chapter one in *Why Worry?* accomplishes the same goals.

Sometimes setting the next appointment can be a challenge. Worriers who are committed to the process and enthusiastic about working with you on their problem will eagerly agree to return. But clients who harbor some hesitancies about the process or who still are unconvinced that these counseling sessions will help them may hesitate to agree to a second session. If necessary, you may have to use your best persuasive skills to encourage the doubtful client to set a day and time for the next session. With some prompting most worriers will agree to return even though their experience with failure when they have tried to change in the past has left them discouraged.

3

The Agony of Worry

The Engagement Stage: Session 2

Scripture and the *Feelings* of Worry

Feelings make a lousy foundation for life and living. While feelings can be wonderful, they can also be very crippling. That is because feelings are fickle. They are adversely affected by everything from the humidity to hormones! Feelings aren't bad, but building your life around them is dangerous. God illustrated the shaky role of feelings and specifically, the feelings associated with worry in Jeremiah 17. Verses 7–10 state, "But blessed is the man who trusts in the LORD, whose confidence is in him. He will be like a tree planted by the water that sends out its roots by the stream. It does not fear when heat comes; its leaves are always green. It has no worries in a year of drought and never fails to bear fruit. The heart is deceitful above all things and beyond cure. Who can understand it? I the LORD search the heart and examine the mind, to reward a man according to his conduct, according to what his deeds deserve." These verses contain some very helpful insights about

63

the feelings of worry. Most importantly, they identify the source of worry and offer some action steps for dealing with them.

The first thing we need to do is define what Jeremiah was talking about when he described the "blessed" person. The word blessed literally meant "to kneel." When blessing God, it was an act of adoration but when applied to people, it meant to receive something from God. A person who was blessed was one who had been the recipient of some divine benefits. In the case of Jeremiah 17 it was the blessing of stability in an unstable world. It was the ability to be worry-free in an envrionment where there was much to worry about. That worry-free mentality was illustrated in the word translated "man." The root of the word used here described a "valiant man" or "warrior." The word picture is quite nice: the blessed individual is one who valiantly addresses life. Jeremiah stated that the ability to cultivate such feelings begins with one's focus.

Notice that the worry-free, "blessed" person is one who has a divine focus rather than a focus on feelings. It says, "*blessed is the man who trusts in the Lord.*" The verse describes a person who looked to the Lord rather than the adverse circumstances of life. It also describes one who has refused to turn inward and throw a first class pity party. Rather, it says that the person's "confidence" was based in the Lord. That is called a focus of faith. You will remember from our previous chapter that faith is the oil in the machinery of life and is vital for worry-free living.

Further, that kind of confident, faith-filled living grants one the ability to actually live better in lean times. As we experience God's provision during adverse circumstances, we learn to trust him more in the future. Worry begins to diminish and we find that our trust grows. That trust feeds our stability and further enables us to function during times of difficulty. Jeremiah described it as having "*no fear when the heat comes*" and "*no worries in the year of drought.*" That is why those who learn to live worry-free often do better in life than those who are crippled by worry. That is also why we must learn to place our confidence in the Lord and cultivate the kind of feelings described by Jeremiah.

Jeremiah went on to say that blessed individuals have "deep roots," meaning that their resources go well beyond themselves and they know it. That resource is the Lord himself. The net result of all this is the countering of fear and the absence of worry. Worry-free individuals are those who have placed not only their focus upon, but their "confidence" in the Lord. The word confidence meant to "find refuge." When your refuge for life is the Lord, you'll find the blessing of worry-free living. While worry-free living may sound impossible to you or your client, the verse clearly says, "*no worries*"—none at all!

The problem we must reckon with is within us: our hearts are deceitful and fraudulent. While all Christians know that they should have a divine focus, our hearts endeavor to trick us into looking elsewhere for stability. That is why Jeremiah said that our hearts are "beyond cure." The word meant feeble or terminal. Left to ourselves our hearts will rob us of peace by filling our emotions with the terminal feelings of fear or hopelessness.

The good news from Jeremiah is that there is hope. He outlined the prescription for dealing with our deceptive hearts: "*I the Lord search the heart and examine the mind.*" God promised that he would help us by intimately examining our hearts and minds. He will help us see through the smoke screens of twisted thinking. When our minds are misdirected toward circumstances, our feelings turn toxic and our peace disappears. God is capable of setting our feelings straight because he is greater than our deceptive hearts. First John 3:19f states it like this: "This then is how we know that we belong to the truth, and how we set our hearts at rest in his presence whenever our hearts condemn us. For God is greater than our hearts . . . " Like Jeremiah, John stated that our hearts can be at rest (in the Lord's presence) when feelings would desire to cripple us. God is able to override them because he is greater. Once again, the determining factor behind the feelings of worry is a faulty focus.

Another passage of Scripture that addresses the feelings of worry is Philippians 4:6–7: "Do not be anxious about anything, but in everything, by prayer and petition, with thanksgiving, present your requests to God. And the peace of God, which transcends all understanding, will guard your hearts and your minds in Christ Jesus." These verses begin with a frighteningly direct command: "*Do not be anxious about anything.*" That does not leave much room for theological "yeah-buts." It is a straightforward command. The standing responsibility of a Christian is to be worry-free. Ideally, we are not permitted to worry about even one thing. While that may sound like an impossible standard, it simply represents the goal toward which we should strive. The war with our feelings is often lost because we convince ourselves that there is no hope. God disagrees and so should we. We need to simply accept his grace when we fail, and then continue to strive toward being the worry-free individuals he has commanded us to be. The question is, is that really possible? I believe God has given us an alternative to the feelings of worry, that alternative is prayer.

While worry is forbidden, prayer is commanded. We have found that prayer is often the first thing Christians talk about and often the last thing they do. Paul was not kidding when he penned those verses and instructed us to pray. He used four different words to emphasize the importance of prayer. The first word referred to prayer as an act of worship. It had nothing to do with asking for things and everything to do with an attitude of praise. It was setting your heart and head straight by focusing upon the Lord's goodness and greatness. When we worship the Lord through our prayers, our focus is redirected back toward God—it's rightful place. The second word Paul used for prayer was translated "petition." It referred to what we typically think of when we talk about prayer. The word emphasized the idea of urgency, it was asking for the things we really need. The third word set the attitude behind our prayer. The word was translated "thanksgiving," and referred to the grateful language offered to God during our prayers. The final word was translated "requests." Like petition, it meant "to ask." Some believe that it referred more to intercessory prayer on behalf of others, whereas "petition" referred to one's personal needs. Without splitting hairs, the meaning is obvious: prayer, all kinds of prayer is the divinely instructed, superior alternative to worry. On the other hand, worry is a human option to prayer.

First Peter 5:7 instructs, *"Cast all your anxiety on him because he cares for you."* So how do you cast your feelings of anxiety and worry upon the Lord? The answer is prayer—all kinds of prayer! The word "cast" is in a Greek tense that means to cast it upon him once and for all. Once an issue is tossed his way you need not worry because "he cares for you." The word "cares" is in a tense that means he never stops caring. The application for us is simply wonderful. We can forget about worrying over something because his undying concern will never allow him to forget!

Now, look back to the Philippians passage. Philippians 4:7 described the outcome of prayer: "And the peace of God, which transcends all understanding, will guard your hearts and your minds in Christ Jesus." That's an amazing promise. Interestingly, it is not a promise to give us all the things we ask for; rather, it is a promise directed toward our feelings and thoughts! When we pray, God will go to work on our feelings. The promise is that the peace of God will guard our hearts and minds. Our entire emotional makeup can be altered, enhanced, or stabilized by the guarding and keeping power of Jesus Christ. Notice that the one doing the guarding is Christ himself! The word "guard" was a colorful military term. It described the role of a sentinel on the wall. His job was to continually scan the horizon for the enemy. Once spotted, the city was alerted to the danger, and the sentinel became a warrior. In this context, our enemy is the worry of our hearts. Christ himself has offered to stand guard over our feelings when we are willing to pray. He has promised both to alert us (our minds) and protect our feelings (our hearts).

The final thought from this passage is connected with the human unreasonableness of the whole concept. The verse described Jesus' supernatural ability to protect our feeling process as "*transcending all understanding.*" The process being described here is not some emotional band-aid or mind-twisting affirmation statements. While it may seem illogical to think that prayer can really affect how one feels, the fact is, God is in the business of doing things that are beyond human comprehension. He is able to provide peace in the place of worry and the avenue through which he has chosen to do so is prayer.

Getting the Client Started

Your second session together should include a review of the goals you set during the previous session. Since this session places the emphasis upon feelings, you'll want to listen carefully for the feelings of your client in regard to the information the two of you shared together. How do they feel about the biblical directive concerning worry? By the end of your previous session they should understand, at least intellectually, the Bible's absolute standard: worry is wrong. Just because the Bible commands it doesn't mean that they have been able to eliminate worry. The issue here is not the standard (that is quite clear); the question is, how do your clients feel about that standard? Are they willing to believe in and, most importantly, feel a willingness to target "worry-free" living as their goal? If they are willing to own the concept, and feel that it is both desirable and obtainable, then growth is possible.

You'll also want to explore their feelings about the statement "faith is the oil in the machinery of life, worry is the sand." How do they feel about faith? What are the road blocks in their feeling process that make faith difficult? Have they been able to feel that worry and faith are mutually exclusive concepts? As you review these concepts from session one, listen for words of their heart. While we hope there has been improvement since our last time together, the only improvement really necessary is that your client feels some hope.

Following this initial probing, ask about the reading assignments you gave them. Which passage of Scripture did they find most meaningful? Which passage was the most difficult to believe? Which verses really stretched them? How did the verses make them feel? What was the most significant feeling that reoccurred? What was the best feeling they experienced? What was the most disturbing feeling? If they could really own one concept from the verses they read, what would it be and why? You will quickly begin to understand the feeling process of your clients as they reflect upon and relate their feelings about Scripture to you.

Once you understand the feelings of your clients, then you can move on to some of the Scriptures used earlier in this chapter. While your session together is not a Bible study, the use of the Bible is vital for real help and healing. Have your clients read through the passage from Jeremiah 17. Ask them something like, "Can you see some benefits to worry-free living?" "What did Jeremiah identify as the major ingredients for worry-free living?" "How does that make you feel?" "What did Jeremiah say was our major problem?" You can certainly add anything you would like about the passage, but the goal is to help them understand that the real enemy is within (our hearts) and that we must look beyond ourselves (to God).

Since the heart is the real problem, have them read 1 John 3:19–20. You'll want to instill hope within them by illustrating the fact that God is greater than the human heart. He can bring the frantic feelings of the human heart under control! You want your clients to walk away today with great hope! Follow up that concept with Philippians 4:6–7. Have them read through it. Ask them what is being commanded. Are there any loopholes in the verses? What is being promised and what is not being promised? You will want to draw them to the conclusion that God is not promising to fix everything that is wrong in life by providing for our every desire, rather he has promised to stand guard over our feelings. How does that make your clients feel?

After talking through some of their feelings and these verses, have them turn to their prayer journal. Have them tell you about the things listed there. Ask them to explain the feelings associated with some of the more important items. Ask them how the study of Philippians 4:6–7 might affect their willingness to pray about the things on their list. Ask them if there are some things that need to be added, deleted, and altered.

Finally, you may want to pray with them or for them. Take their list and pray through the list with them. Model how they should pray. Help them to see how you pass the things listed on to their Heavenly Father. Try to identify with their feelings and pray as you would if the list were your very own. Remember, the goal today is for feelings of hope to replace the feelings of anxiety.

Responding to Feelings

The Strategic Pastoral Counselor's major task in this second session is to encourage the exploration of feelings. While this task can sometimes be difficult for the counselee, counselors also can struggle with feelings. Many of us have gathered some unhelpful attitudes about feelings. Well-meaning authors will sometimes write that the reason emotionally disturbed people struggle so much is that they already pay too much attention to their feelings. Thus, some would say, we should not encourage any exploration of feelings because such an approach would not be helpful.

Dr. Benner in his book *Strategic Pastoral Counseling* has outlined for us the value of attending to the affective side of our counselees' struggles. This strategy is particularly appropriate for worriers because they bring to the counseling process a host of unexamined emotions, emotions that they must begin to face more directly if they are ever to escape from the clutches of their worry patterns.

Dr. Borkovec has identified many of the emotions that worriers encounter while worrying: anxiety, tension, apprehensiveness, frustration, and dread. Worriers most often focus on the thought content running through their minds during their worry times, and they may only be vaguely aware of the attendant emotions that accompany the process. By helping worriers identify concurrent emotions, you will help them establish the negative quality of worry and its potential destructiveness.

We know that the worry process already contains sufficient quantities of avoidance. Worriers do not need to add the avoidance of worry to their list of already avoided items. We need to help them face their emotions directly and not avoid them. For example, if the cognitive worry process has become a way to avoid the feeling of apprehension that the worrier would otherwise feel, we can help remove some of the "necessity" for worry by helping the worrier face the apprehension directly. When the worrier realizes the apprehension is not all that awful to experience, some of the power of the apprehension to drive the worry process will diminish.

When working with the feelings of clients, counselors can respond in helpful and unhelpful ways. Unhelpful responses include comments that are perhaps accurate but terribly premature. For example, worriers may describe feelings of apprehension. If the pastoral counselor should immediately say, "Well, those feelings are totally out of line for the believer who is to be filled at all times with God's peace," the response will be primarily unhelpful. We want to move our clients toward being able to replace their apprehension with God's peace. This change is a growth goal, however, and not an immediate expectation.

You respond helpfully to feelings when you respond with comments that reassure clients you have accurately heard them and that you still care about them even though they experience these feelings. Worriers will be able to trust you more completely when they know that what they tell you will not elicit from you scorn, rejection, or contempt.

Some counselors may feel high levels of discomfort when counselees express strong feeling. Pastoral counselors must develop the ability to be present with counselees even when they are dealing with intense and powerful feelings. Only then will we function adequately as listeners.

Problems You May Encounter

We have already mentioned problems that can occur during the first session. Yet another set of concerns can arise during the second counseling session. If your counselee felt encouraged after the initial visit, qualms regarding the second visit may never appear. But if problems do develop regarding this second session, they may fall into one of the following categories.

Adverse Reactions to Session One

Some people will feel a mild sense of euphoria after an initial visit that will evaporate in the interval between sessions. Clients can build up a sense of hope based on reassurances the counselor has given only to find that subsequent struggles with worry are as strong as ever. When problems do not disappear or remit as quickly as we would like, we all experience discouragement. If you sense that a counselee is having just such a reaction, or, better yet, if the counselee is able to describe such feelings to you, you can be of help by repeating our guidelines. Change is a process; God does not always choose to change us immediately; many people feel this way when just beginning counseling.

Another adverse reaction to the first session can occur when counselees lose confidence in your counseling skills. Perhaps they question whether you truly are using a Bible-based approach to their worry problem. Perhaps you sounded too "psychological" when you gave them homework assignments that included activities other than Bible reading or memory. Or perhaps the opposite has occurred. Some counselees react adversely to too many references to God, the Bible, or to prayer. In each of these instances, we must balance our interventions carefully between the "psychological" and the "spiritual" in accord with the spiritual maturation levels of our clients. Sometimes we develop this sensitivity to the client's individual situation only by trial and error.

Finally, you may occasionally see a counselee who will react negatively to the first counseling session because of a subconscious determination not to improve. This reaction is rare because most counselees genuinely want relief from the troubling thoughts of worry. However, as we have seen in the introductory chapter, worry can be a pattern of behavior that covers some more profound struggles. As long as the worry system continues, the counselee does not have to fear that the underlying issues will surface. So when an effective pastoral counselor begins to help unravel the grip of worry on such a counselee's life, that very effectiveness can signal subconscious forces to resist the help. Because this reaction is rare, pastoral counselors will not encounter this situation frequently. Counselees who do show this pattern will need referral, a counseling skill we will discuss later in this book.

Struggles with Session Two

When the pastoral counselor seeks to help clients express feelings, several difficulties can emerge. Many people are well equipped to use logic and reason and at the same time may be very poorly equipped to process feelings. In some cases this pattern may be longstanding, the result of strong socializing pressures in this direction. Sometimes the church has reinforced these tendencies by glorifying the importance of thinking and debunking the value of feeling. Using Philippians 4:8 as a proof text, some Bible teachers have maintained that correct thinking is all we need to face life's problems.

A biblically balanced viewpoint toward emotions, however, recognizes that God created all aspects of human functioning and that they were very good (Gen. 1:31). God created feelings as much as he created the other domains of human functioning. God wishes us to live lives with our emotional life rich and healthy as illustrated by the fruit of the Spirit in Galatians 5. He created us whole people designed to function with wholeness as our major characteristic. We cannot derogate what God has created. Feelings, just as the will, the intellect, and cognition, must be dedicated to God's glory and must be under his sovereign control. Feelings can deceive, just as the intellect, will, and cognition functions can deceive. But if we are going to say that feelings are totally unreliable and therefore not worthy of attention in counseling, we will have to base that assertion on personal prejudice, not Scripture.

Counselees may also suffer from a common malady that interferes with the free expression or description of emotions. Males and not a few females can have difficulty knowing and verbalizing exactly what they are feeling. Counselees may need some extra help from you during this session to enumerate the various emotions that accompany their worry processes. Remember, the value in prompting our clients to describe these feelings to us is that the experience will set the stage for a full treatment of their worry problem. Our goal is to alleviate worry on affective as well as on cognitive and behavioral levels.

Occasionally the counselor will see and hear a certain emotion as a client speaks, but the counselee gives no evidence of recognizing any such feeling. And when the perceptive pastoral counselor gently speculates, "Sounds like you are somewhat terrified by that prospect," the client can vehemently deny having any such feeling. Such denial is not a proper trigger for an argument. Your client's response merely indicates that she or he is not yet ready to face what may be very obvious to everyone else around.

Resistance

All good counseling eventually encounters resistance. Long-term or short-term counseling is not always easy sailing, even with very cooperative clients. Resistance will often appear just when the process is beginning to produce effective results. In the case of short-term counseling, such as the model you are following with your worry clients, resistance may appear quite early in the five-session format.

How can you recognize resistance? When the client hesitates to agree with the most obvious of reflections, or when the client refuses to agree to the next logical step in the healing process. Resistance is a natural feeling on behalf of a client who is in counseling, and the effective pastoral counselor should not use this outcropping of negativity as an occasion to enter a power struggle or to launch a major campaign to convince. Instead we should recognize mile signs of resistance as signals that we are perhaps moving a bit too quickly or that we should back off to give the threatened counselee a little more emotional room in the process.

None of the problems you may encounter in session two are monumental. They simply may challenge your skill as a creative healer. With God's help none of these stumbling blocks need prove fatal to the counseling process.

New Perspectives and Coping Strategies

Worriers will only find relief when they replace their worry patterns with new perspectives and coping strategies. Our goal as pastoral counselors is not to eliminate a bothersome behavior but to replace that behavioral pattern with a more God-honoring approach to future events.

We want to outline in this section some of those new approaches that we will want our counselees to adopt. These strategies will not only facilitate the beginning phases of change from worry to peaceful frames of mind, they will eventually replace long-standing worry patterns. We are convinced that the new perspectives we discuss in this section will be the basis on which the Holy Spirit will assist the worrier in building new feelings, cognitions, and behaviors.

Before we enumerate these replacement patterns, we must distinguish them from self-talk. Cognitive theories of therapy seek to help clients replace incorrect thinking with new thoughts that will produce better mental health. In this case the emphasis is on cognition and thinking. We feel that the replacement strategies must be far more than just new thoughts. These new perspectives and coping strategies need to be fully-developed healing avenues that provide the basis for new feelings and behaviors as well as new thoughts. Thus we are introducing these concepts while discussing session two even though they will have many implications for all three sessions in the engagement phase.

The following perspectives then comprise the replacements we trust our worriers can adopt.

I Am Not Alone

If worriers do not know they are not alone, they need to know. Others have struggled with the same agonies, and others have also conquered the most serious forms of worry. Friends and family are supportive of the worrier's efforts to contain the problem. The worrier is not alone.

Jesus is with the worrier. "Surely I am with you always, even to the very end of the age" (Matt. 28:20b) are words of great comfort to every worrier. Jesus is a companion to us as we struggle with life's challenges. He understands our struggles and can empathize with us as no other human can. "For we do not have a high priest who is unable to sympathize with our weaknesses, but we have one who has been tempted in every way, just as we are—yet without sin" (Heb. 4:15).

Did Jesus worry? Some people are hesitant to believe that Jesus worried or was ever anxious. Yet the teaching of Hebrews suggests that Jesus experienced all points of human weakness but never entered into sin as do all of us. The graphic descriptions of Jesus in the Garden of Gethsemane make us think of apprehension, dread, and anxiety. Did Jesus worry about his impending death? Perhaps. We can confidently say, however, that Jesus does know from experience the pain and agony of having to face the future with its negative reality. Jesus did not exaggerate the negative probabilities of his future, but he did know personally about the experience of having to face the future. Whether or not he worried about the future may be a matter of semantics; we do know for certain that he did not sin as he struggled with what the future held for him. He can be an empathic companion to the worrier who consciously realizes Christ's never-failing presence with us.

Like Christ, we must face our dread and apprehension of the future. The technical term for this approach is exposure. Worriers will profit from exposing themselves to their dread and anxiety just as Jesus did. Worriers are not alone; Christ is with them as their example in facing this baffling human problem.

A Growth Opportunity

We can view our struggles negatively or as opportunities for growth. Worriers are likely to feel discouragement that their bothersome patterns of fretting have pushed them toward pastoral counseling. Most of us would prefer not to have problems such as chronic worry. Yet we can benefit by adopting a perspective that helps us see these encounters with our imperfection as opportunities to grow and mature.

As pastoral counselors we must create an expectation among our worrying clients that, with God's help, they will see improvement as a result of our work together. Further, we want this improvement to link up with general patterns of growth and development that are occurring in the worrier's life. If the worrier is not aware of ongoing processes of maturation in Christ, we need to address this issue with the client. Facing our problems is not an admission of failure but a commitment to pursue Christlikeness and growth in our spiritual lives.

The Use of Faith

Pastoral counselors must help the worrying clients learn the teaching of Scripture regarding worry. Knowing what the Bible says about this or any other topic, however, is insufficient impetus for change. We must call on the Holy Spirit to energize these truths (one side of the coin), and we must actively exercise faith to incorporate these truths into our lives (the other side of the coin). Knowing truth puts content into our heads. With the use of faith and reliance on the Holy Spirit we must move that truth into our souls and hearts.

Faith faces problems directly. Faith says, "On the basis of what Christ has done for me in the past, I will step out into new arenas of God's care for me." Faith marches into problems; faith abandons the pattern of avoidance that worriers have so effectively used over time.

When we can help the worrier adopt such a proactive and energized perspective for tackling the worry problem, we will have helped them take a major step toward healing. Growth in Christ comes when we renew our commitments to growth and when we allow God's spirit to produce that growth in us.

Peace, Worry's Antidote

Peace is God's good gift to all worriers. Peace is the antidote to worry. If we are peaceful, we are not worrying; if we worry, we do not have peace. The peace that Jesus promises us is unmatched by any other human experience. Carl F. H. Henry has well described that peace.

> A peace that can look beyond the terrors of crucifixion to resurrection morning—a peace that can see in the very death of the cross itself God's victory over all that would put an end to Christ's cause, and the conquest of death itself—is a peace adequate for any exigency that you or I will ever be called upon to face (Henry 1987, 27).

Peace is an essential part of the fruit that the Holy Spirit seeks to produce in our lives. Paul wrote,

> Do not be anxious about anything, but in everything, by prayer and petition, with thanksgiving, present your requests to God. And the peace of God, which transcends all understanding will guard your hearts and your minds in Christ Jesus (Phil. 4:6–7).

We obtain peace through prayer. Prayer itself calms us. No one can worry while praying. In response to these prayers for help, God will bring to us a peace that cannot be fully understood but which will replace our worry.

New Time Perspectives

We have seen how the worrier allows anticipation of the future and regret over the past to ruin the present. The Bible teaches us that Christians need to form a balanced time perspective, one that carefully keeps all three major components of time in proper relationship. The worrier, if s/he is to experience any relief from worry, will have to adjust how the past and the future interact with the present.

Regarding the past, the Bible tells us to remember the past, to learn from it, but not to harbor bitterness, revenge, or regret from the past. Regarding the future, the Bible tells us to be prepared, to live in the present with the future in view, and to exercise faith regarding the uncertainties of the future. Helping our worrisome clients develop a biblical attitude toward the present, past, and future may be one of the most significant new perspectives we can help them build.

Community

Worry is a lonely struggle. Because the fretting patterns often involve private, internalized speech, the worrier can become increasingly isolated from others. As more and more of the worrier's connections with a healthy Christian community are severed, potential healing resources for the worrier likewise disappear. Worriers need to reconnect with believers. They need to experience renewed contact with a Christian community.

Helping worriers form this new perspective may prove to be the counselor's greatest challenge. Introverted or otherwise isolated worriers will resist expanding their world to include more people. They may not wish to join an accountability group that can help them solidify their gains against the ongoing struggle with worry. They may not wish to abandon the "security" of aloneness for the risk of group participation. However, we know from Scripture that the body of Christ is uniquely designed to be a healing, supportive community. If we can help our worrying clients adopt a commitment to that healing community, we will have served them well.

Preparing for Session Three

In preparation for your third session, have your client review the concepts of your time together. Ask them what they have heard you say. See if they can put the content into three or four sentences. Ask them to summarize how they feel at this point. You might want them to put their feelings into single words like "hopeful" or "anxious." The point is to bring closure to your conversation and help your client reduce the information to a memorable level.

If you are using the *Why Worry?* booklet, you'll want to remind them to work through the next section. You might want to have them read through the passages of Scripture the two of you covered during this session. If answering the generic questions we described on page 60 (chapter 2) worked well for them, you may want them to repeat the exercise using the Scriptures that were related to worry.

Since prayer is the biblical formula for healing our feelings, encourage them to use their prayer list daily. Let them know that prayer does not need to occupy huge blocks of time. Some avoid praying because they don't feel they have the time necessary for prayer. Encourage them to spend three or four minutes a couple of times a day in concentrated prayer. When they see the benefits they may find more time for praying, but for now, just encourage them to get started or keep going.

Finally, set up a time for your next appointment, encourage them to work diligently, and leave them with hope!

4

Worrying about Worry

The Engagement Stage: Session 3

Scripture and the *Thoughts* of Worry

Feelings of worry are often elusive and unpredictable. They can arrive in your heart without much warning. The Scripture we explored in our last session identified the source of those feelings and prescribed a biblical defense against them. We are instructed to allow Jesus Christ to stand guard over our hearts by taking our concerns to him in prayer. This session, our focus is upon the thoughts associated with worry. Our thinking process is the indispensable basis for effectively curtailing worry. When the feelings of worry assault us, our minds are capable of determining what to do with those feelings. We can counter them with truth or our thoughts can enhance them. When our thoughts amplify and intensify the feelings of worry, our thinking has turned toxic.

Worry is thinking turned toxic. Worry is allowing concern to degenerate into poisonous thoughts. It is as if worry cuts a channel in your mind through which all other thoughts are drained. That results in a loss of objectivity and leaves us crippled. Jesus knew

81

just how paralyzing worry could be. He made a fascinating statement in Luke 21:14–15: "But make up your mind not to worry beforehand how you will defend yourselves. For I will give you words and wisdom that none of your adversaries will be able to resist or contradict." Jesus' statement aggressively confronts toxic thinking.

The first issue in this passage is a command: "*but make up your mind not to worry . . .*" Since God would not ask us to do the impossible, apparently our minds can choose whether we will worry or not. Since we have an option, Jesus said that we should opt for the "not to worry" track. The phrase "make up" is a translation from a word that means "to premeditate." Thoughts are a rehearsal for real life. By saying "make up your mind," Jesus laid the groundwork for a rehearsal of thoughts that intentionally excluded worry. We must cultivate a mind-set that refuses to entertain thoughts of worry. Worry is simply not an option. When the thoughts of worry come our way, we are to expel them. While that may sound impossible, chances are you already do it in many areas of life. For example, when thoughts of stealing something pops into your mind, what do you do? Do you nurse those thoughts, allowing your imagination to run wild? Of course not, by an act of your will you expel them as ridiculous. When lusty thoughts come to mind, believers do not typically dwell on them for long periods of time—we know that to do so would be sin. We set those thoughts aside and get on with life because we know the thoughts are wrong and that nothing good can come from them. Likewise, dwelling upon, cultivating, enhancing, and tolerating thoughts of worry is equally wrong and equally destructive. That is why Jesus made the outlandish statement, "Make up your mind not to worry." Worrisome thoughts are a choice!

The second issue of interest in this verse revolves around the promise Jesus made. That promise was the reason why his followers could put aside the thoughts of worry. Verse 15 says, "*For I will give you words and wisdom . . .*" That is a great promise for a worried group of people. What more could anyone ask for? We do not need to worry about the words we will say tomorrow because he has promised to give us the words we need. We need not worry about the decisions of tomorrow, for he has promised to give us wisdom. The verse is certainly not advocating laziness or a lack of preparation for the future, but the principle is very clear: God will provide. One contemporary study after another cites public speaking as people's number one fear. Think about it, Jesus took on humanity's number one worry and said, "Don't worry, I'll help you to know what to say." Who among us hasn't wished they could peek into tomorrow so we could make the right decision today? Jesus said, "Don't worry, I'll give you all the wisdom you need when you need it. What more do you want?"

Another verse addressing thoughts of worry is Philippians 4:8–9. The context is worry. In the previous chapter we discussed the role of verses six and seven in our feeling process. Now, in verses eight and nine, God has turned from worrisome feelings to worrisome thoughts. Philippians 4:8–9 states: "Finally, brothers, whatever is true, whatever is noble, whatever is right, whatever is pure, whatever is lovely, whatever is admirable—if anything is excellent or praiseworthy—think about such things. Whatever you have learned or received or heard from me, or seen in me—put it into practice. And the God of peace will be with you." Just as prayer will protect your heart from worry (verses 6–7), the right mind-set will guarantee that the God of peace will continue to stand guard over your heart. Sometimes we unknowingly relieve him of duty by flirting with unhealthy, faith-wrenching thoughts. Let us show you what we mean.

First, notice that the responsibility for our thoughts rests with us. It is our obligation to guard our minds carefully. God says he will guard our hearts, but we must guard our minds. What does it mean to guard your mind? It means that we are to screen carefully the raw material we put into our system of thought. The old computer saying goes like this: "Garbage in, garbage out." It is not only true for computers, it is also true for the human thought process. Our feelings tend to revolve around the focus of our thoughts. Whatever gets our attention ultimately gets us. That is why we get that queasy feeling of falling when we walk up to a cliff and look over the edge. Likewise, we worry more when we have pumped our minds full of negative information.

In the Philippians passage, Paul suggested an impressive list of the things that should fill our minds. At the end of the list he simply said, "think about such things." The word translated "think" meant "to take an inventory." One of the prerequisites to winning the war with worry is to take an inventory of the things we put into our minds. What would taking such an inventory reveal about your thoughts? What kind of information are you feeding into your thought process? Would they measure up to the standard set in verse eight? Probably not for many of us—but if you are struggling with worry, you simply cannot compromise at this point. To do so is to feed the monster we are trying to kill!

Paul said our minds should be directed toward the things that are "true," and "noble." The word "noble" meant things that were straightforward and honorable. Paul said our minds should rest upon things that are "right." The word meant that which is "innocent or holy." He continued with the word "pure." It was a reference to the things that were "modest, morally clean and chaste." He also included the words "lovely" and "admirable." The word admirable referred to the things that had an "excellent reputation." He continued his directive with the word "excellent," a word that was closely tied with manliness and the idea of valor. You might think of it as the classic idea of chivalry. The final word used by Paul was "praiseworthy." This word referred to things that made you want to applaud. It was not the kind of courteous applause that we often feel obligated to render in order to be polite. This was the kind of response that stands you on your feet and drives your hands together in a thunderous standing ovation! That is quite a list. The question is, how does your reading material fare in comparison? How do the movies and videos you watch measure up against Paul's list of "peace producers"?

As noteworthy and complete as Paul's list may be, it is remarkable that the list doesn't contain a hint of evil or things with questionable character. That is because anything less often sets our minds to spinning. Here is what we mean. Consider the housewife who immerses her mind in a racy romance novel about infidelity. Then, for some strange reason she begins to worry about her husband's faithfulness. She might also start to worry about their relationship since it doesn't seem to have the passion illustrated in the book. Consider the teenager who watches some slasher film and then begins to worry about being attacked. Just seeing the movie commercials for "Chucky," (a film about a demon-possessed doll) caused our son to worry about his talking doll friend "Corky." Five years later Corky was still confined to our bedroom because none of the kids wanted him around—just in case! Consider the businessperson who reads of nothing but "doom and gloom" about the economy. He will quite likely find himself worrying at night about the future of his business instead of creatively dreaming about how to take advantage of the current economy. Is it any wonder that we worry when we watch the news twice a day, read the paper, scan the headlines, watch "Rescue 911," and end our day with an unhealthy overdose of CNN Headline News? We pump so much negative reality and media-induced horror into our minds that we begin to worry about our future. Its a wonder that more of us don't snap.

Not only do we have to contend with the media, but our own firsthand experiences sometimes confirm our worrisome fears. During a single month, my wife Sonya and I learned that still another close friends' marriage was splitting up. A young mother in our church found out she had cancer. A young family we know was in a terrible car wreck, the teenage son of a friend is into serious rebellion, and one of our daughter's junior high teachers murdered three people during summer vacation! With all the tragic things that occur around us, we are often left worrying, "Am I next?" That is why worriers need to carefully guard and limit the input.

One last verse illustrates the proper focus of our thoughts. Hebrews 12:2 reads: "Let us fix our eyes on Jesus, the author and perfecter of our faith." Rather than focusing our thoughts upon the worrisome circumstances of this present world, we must fix our thoughts upon Jesus. Since he has promised to give us both words and wisdom, then why not look to him when life is uncertain? He is the author and perfecter of our faith. That means that Jesus got our faith going and he will help our faith to grow if we will fix our focus upon him.

Checking on the Progress

At the beginning of your third session you'll want to check on your client's outside work. Review their workbook and look for anything that shows signs of improvement or hope. Ask a few strategic questions that might bring some progress to the forefront of their thoughts.

Look through their prayer list. Are there any answers to prayer that should be acknowledged? You might find that some of the things listed on the early part of the list (two weeks ago) were time related, meaning that they are no longer an issue of worry because they simply didn't happen or God turned them into something constructive. For example, let's assume that they listed "Worried about the mole on my shoulder." Since then, they have been to the doctor, the mole was removed and the test results were benign. Help them to see that worry was a fruitless exercise since they had nothing to worry about. On the other hand, suppose the mole was malignant and their fears were confirmed. Does that mean that worry was justified? Did worry contribute anything constructive to the situation? Of course not, and they need to understand that. They must see that prayer and going to the doctor were far more sensible measures than worrying. You can help them celebrate the fact that the mole was discovered and removed.

You are probing for progress. Hopefully, by this time, they will be able to identify some areas of improvement. However, improvement is often difficult for us to see within ourselves. One of the most important jobs you have as their counselor, is to help them see, feel, and celebrate the progress that is being made. When they feel like they are moving forward, their desire, hope, and efforts will begin to snowball. You must help them uncover the growth within their life. By now, you'll know some areas where they are prone to worry. Ask them about those areas and have them give you some specific examples from the week. If they have made good progress, it might be difficult for them to pinpoint improvement because they didn't worry like they might have in the past. Helping them see any circumstance during the week when they could have or should have worried but did not is a major victory that you will want to celebrate with your words of encouragement.

Another way to check up on the progress of your clients is to ask if their family or friends have made any constructive comments. Little comments can speak volumes about progress and your client's need to reflect upon and enjoy them. During the past week did they hear anything like, "You seem more relaxed," "You really handled that well," or "I sure enjoyed today with you." If others, especially family and friends, are making positive comments, you have reason to celebrate!

You'll also want to ask about the failures of the previous week. What one area really plagued them? Ask them to give you a specific example of a time when worry got a grip. Have them explain how they felt and how they responded to those feelings. Did they pray? Did they see the potential for worry coming or did it roar into their lives without any warning? As you talk through this, it's crucial that they sense understanding and acceptance from you. You need not be critical or judgmental. Chances are, their own conscience and feelings of failure will be heaping enough guilt their way. Smile, and let them know that you understand. The chances are, pastor, you have been there too!

The object behind exploring an area of failure is not to convey disapproval, nor to bolster your feeling of being needed. The goal here is to convey the grace of God to your clients. They need to hear and feel that failure is not the end of the world. They need to understand that God isn't mad or even disappointed. An illustration I often use with people might prove helpful. It was an exciting week when my children decided it was time to take their first steps. As parents, those steps meant so much to us. I remember each child wobbling, unsure, catching the table for stability, and then, the first step. Wow, it was a wonderful sight, you would think my kid had just won a gold medal! That is how God feels when we make an effort at growth. Following those first few steps was the inevitable fall. I'd tell them how proud I was and encouraged them to get up and keep going, so does God. Never once did I say or think, "You good-for-nothing, uncoordinated kid, you'll never learn to walk!" God does not have those thoughts either. He loves and accepts people. He honors and encourages effort. He is a gracious supporter, even when we fail.

Monitoring Thoughts

The human thinking process is a marvel of God's creative hand. Psychologists have studied the phenomenon extensively during the twentieth century. Although we still do not fully understand the human process of thinking, what we do know convinces us that human thinking is central to our functioning and well-being.

Observers have known for centuries that humans engage in thinking and that a major portion of the thinking process occurs in patterns of silent speech. In essence we have silent conversations with ourselves. These private talks help us plan our activities, make decisions, function on a daily basis. This feature of thinking occurs automatically and is often subconscious or just beyond our direct awareness. When we deliberately focus on our internal speech we can become very aware and conscious of it.

These thought processes are at the heart of our concerns with worrying clients. We have already seen how important thinking is to worriers. We also know that some thought occurs in the form of images, not merely words. Research indicates that some worriers use images as at least part of their worrying process in addition to the prevalence of unspoken words.

Learning theorists are not the only professionals who study the phenomenon of thinking. Clinicians have also generated an interest in internal thought. We have discovered that the thinking patterns of distressed and disturbed persons differs greatly from the thought patterns of people not beset with emotional disorder. In addition, we know that altering those internal thought processes can have a profound impact on the recovery and restoration of emotional well-being.

A major task we have in this session involves helping our worriers monitor their thoughts and internal speech. These clients will already be aware of their internal speech so they will respond cooperatively when we ask them to begin noticing the thoughts that race through their minds, especially when they are worrying.

After clients are aware of their thoughts, they need next to begin recording the exact content of those thoughts in a journal. The very task of capturing a thought and writing the thought down will interrupt the thinking/worrying process. When clients discover that they can exercise some control over the process we have helped them take a giant step toward improvement. Clients who are using *Why Worry?* will find exercises there that aim to help them record their thought patterns while worrying.

When clients bring these worry journals to a counseling session, the pastoral counselor can utilize the material in one or both of two ways. First, the counselor can read over the journal making observations and summary comments that will help the counselee understand the worry patterns. Or, second, the counselor can ask the client to glance over the written journal and to summarize for the counselor the patterns that seem to be present in the recorded thoughts. The advantage of utilizing this latter strategy is obvious: clients get themselves involved in sorting out their individual worry patterns.

In the next section we want to examine the typical kinds of thoughts that you and your clients are likely to discover as you examine these worry journals.

The Importance of Thinking

In this session with our worrying client we must expose the faulty beliefs that attend the worrying process. These beliefs have accrued over the years. Worriers will not immediately recognize the following misbeliefs as their own because some of them are logical extensions of their worrying patterns. But when you as a pastoral counselor expose these implicit beliefs to worriers, they will be able to understand how these thoughts have indeed played a central role in their worrying patterns.

Typical Misbeliefs

The following list of misbeliefs is suggestive rather than exhaustive. Your client may have developed additional destructive thoughts. In each case "X" is some event in the future.

The occurrence of X is a high probability. Worriers would not waste the time they do on future events if such a misbelief did not coexist with the worry. Friends of the worrier will take a very different approach to the very same future event by attaching a low probability to its occurrence. Helping worriers understand the faulty estimation regarding probability is a first step toward unraveling the bothersome knot of worry. Often an effective means the counselor can use to accomplish such a goal is to ask worriers to list all the future events they have worried about in the last year. When worriers answer the counselor's question, "And how many of these events actually happened?" they may be able to see how badly they are misguessing probabilities.

If X happens, the results will be negative, very negative in fact. Worrying is different from the lottery ticket holder who is sure of a future jackpot. Worrying involves imagined negative outcomes. Even if some of these dreaded happenings should actually occur, the realistic outcome is often very mild indeed when compared to what the worrier anticipated. To expose this thinking error, the pastoral counselor will want to find out why the worrier so often dreads such a negative outcome. Did significant family members in their background think this negatively? Do most other people around them think this negatively? Did Jesus think this negatively about his future while here on earth? These and other questions may help the worrier see the futility of this false belief.

I must worry about X so I am prepared for what will happen. The truth is that the worrier prepares the self for a single outcome or two that have very low probability of happening. In the process the worrier is unprepared for the other 99 percent of the outcomes that are more likely to occur. As we have seen earlier, this attempt by worriers to be prepared probably stems from some embarrassing event in the past. Worriers could have wrongly concluded at that time, using available childlike logic, that "If we had only anticipated this embarrassment, we could have avoided the problem." This thinking is false and unhelpful. A variant of this misbelief is, "If we worry about X, then it will not happen." This misbelief is even more primitive and childlike. Worriers need to rethink these assumptions, this time using adult reasoning and thinking abilities. Most worriers are able to use higher levels of reasoning and logic in most other areas of their lives. We are just challenging them now in their counseling to extend these healthy thinking patterns to their worrying.

Worrying about X is better than doing something about it. Worriers have made the choice to think about future events rather than doing something about them. When we deal with behavior in our fourth session with the worrier, we will attend specifically to this matter. In general, we will want to help the worrier find behaviors in the form of preventive actions that will replace the worrying process. For example, if the worrier is afraid of arriving late for an important engagement, we will help the worrier make sure the proper starting time is correctly entered in a datebook and that time in advance of the engagement is kept clear of responsibilities that might interfere with promptness. These preventive actions and behaviors will eventually replace the endless worrisome thoughts.

Catastrophizing Thoughts

Worriers allow their thinking to spiral into ever-increasing levels of dread. The end results of such catastrophizing are so far removed from the originating worry that the connections are sometimes difficult to make between the two. The following is but one example of how these catastrophizing patterns can work:

1. If I am late for that meeting at work, the boss and everyone else will notice.
2. When the boss sees that I am late, she will be upset and will remember the event when she writes my next annual review.
3. Then my review will not go well and I will miss the next pay raise that my family needs.
4. Without the pay raise we will not be able to save any money for the new roof our house badly needs.
5. The value of our house will then go down so we will not be able to obtain that second mortgage that we will need to send our son to college.
6. If he does not get to go to college, he will have to take a job similar to mine and his life will be ruined.
7. And because my son's life will be ruined, I will be a failure at parenting just like I've been a failure at everything else I've ever tried to do.
8. I'm worth nothing.

All of this misery can be generated by what for most people is just a passing thought: "What if I am late for that meeting at work?" This catastrophizing process obviously makes simple worry a beastly affair of the mind. As pastoral counselors we want to help

worriers identify their tendencies to catastrophize and to intervene
early in the process so that the worrier can contain the process.

Strategies for Session Three

What can the counselor do to help the worrier break up these
disabling patterns? Here are four goals you will want to achieve
with your worrying client.

Expose their false beliefs. The false beliefs listed above thrive
when they are subtle and covert. Brought to the light of reason they
lose their power to hold worriers captive. Bringing these implicit
beliefs to the attention of worriers will help weaken their impact
on how they see the future.

Decatastrophize the worry process. The counselor can lead the
worrier through a series of "What if . . . ?" questions. What if you
are late for the meeting at work? What if your boss remembers the
event at the time of your next annual review? By using this line of
pursuit, the counselor will elicit the major steps in the worrier's
catastrophizing process. Worriers are known to have more elaborate catastrophizing scenarios than do nonworriers who are
prompted to imagine the worst about some future event. Pursuing
the negative consequences to their very worst possible outcome
will help clients "touch bottom." If the very worst outcome is that
I will die, is that an impossible outcome for me as a believer to face?
Of course not. When we discover that we could handle the very
worst outcome, should that unlikely development actually happen,
we take the sting out of the entire worry process.

Change to "Even if" statements. The next step in helping free
the worrier from these bothersome patterns is to help them con-
vert their "What if?" questions to "Even if" statements. The believer
is called on to exhibit courage. When we can live out that courage,
even in the face of events about which we normally worry a great
deal, we are living lives that please God. "Even if I do not get that
next scheduled raise, God will continue to be our faithful provider."
"Even if we cannot get a sizable second mortgage to finance our
son's college education, God will help us discover some other
means of sending him to school." These "even if" statements
become for the worrier a declaration of faith in the providential

care of a loving heavenly Father no matter what might happen in the future.

Anchor these changes in Scripture. As you encourage worriers to change their imprisoning patterns of worry, you can confidently advocate these changes on the basis of truths in God's word that we now want to review.

New Perspectives and Coping Strategies

Showing your client how to anchor change to Scripture is the goal of this section. Nothing has the power to change one's thoughts like the word of God. That's because God's word is more than idle print on the page, it is alive. It has the ability to touch and change us. Hebrews 4:12 states: "For the word of God is living and active. Sharper than any double-edged sword, it penetrates even to dividing soul and spirit, joints and marrow; it judges the thoughts and attitudes of the heart." The word translated "active" is the word from which we get the English word "energize." The Bible is able to energize us for change. It has an amazing ability to cut through all the smoke and mirrors that we often throw up in order to protect ourselves from hardcore truth. The Bible is like a mirror directed at the human heart. It has the ability to reveal and impact our attitudes and thoughts. Once the word is within us, it can effect real change! If your clients understand this, it will help them to buy into the following coping strategy.

The Scriptures command us to take every thought captive. Our thoughts are not to spin out of control; rather, we are to captivate them. Second Corinthians 10:5 states: "We demolish arguments and every pretension that sets itself up against the knowledge of God, and we take captive every thought to make it obedient to Christ." When worry assaults us with all kinds of pretentious arguments, we are to take those arguments and confront them directly with Scripture. Worriers tend to develop thoughts rather than demolish them. We are to capture them and make them obedient to Christ. Since we already know that God forbids worrisome thoughts, the question before us is how to take those thoughts captive rather than being captivated.

First we need to realize that capturing thoughts is a real possibility. Remind your clients that God would not ask them to do the impossible. Since he has commanded us to capture our thoughts, it is certainly possible to do so.

Second, we must understand that God wants to replace our anxiety with joy. Psalms 94:19 says, "When anxiety was great within me, your consolation brought joy to my soul." God is not playing "hide-and-seek" with people. He genuinely wants to provide consolation for the soul and especially when anxiety peaks within our lives!

Third, the secret to captivating our thoughts and making them obedient to Christ rests not with us, but rather with the transforming power of the Scriptures. In Matthew 13, Jesus described what can happen by the transforming power of the word of God. He told the story of a farmer who tossed some seed into a field. Some of the seed fell among thorns and was choked out. When asked to explain the parable, Jesus said that the seed was the word of God and that the weeds represented the worries of life. The weed-infested soil illustrated how people can allow the worries of the world to choke out the productivity of the word within them.

Sometimes during a counseling session, your clients will light up inside as they connect with a relevant truth from the Scriptures. Unfortunately, when they leave your office, the worries of life come back in full force and strangle out the life-changing potential of the Scriptures. The problem does not rest with the Scriptures, the deficiency is our personal tolerance for the weeds of worry within our lives. Captivating our thoughts and bringing them into obedience of Christ will only occur when we embrace the Scriptures the same way we have internalized the patterns of worry.

David once wrote, "I have hidden your word in my heart that I might not sin against you" (Ps. 119:11). Our task, as believers, is to internalize the Scriptures so they can transform us. As we learn to implant them within our hearts, the weeds of worry will be choked out. A casual reading, or a flippant, "Oh yeah, I've heard that before" doesn't qualify for hiding the word within your heart, and it certainly won't produce life change. The word translated "hide" meant to not only "hide by covering something over," but "to hoard and protect." The idea was to value something so much that you constantly protected it from theft by hiding or hoarding it. We need to place that kind of premium upon the word of God within our hearts. Once such a value system is embraced by your clients they will be ready for the action step.

The action step begins with the selection of specific Scriptures that have been meaningful to your client. Ideally, your clients should select three or four verses from the homework they have been doing in conjunction with your counseling sessions. Since worry is the subject, the verses need to relate directly to the issue of worry. Once the verses have been selected, have your clients write them out on small cards. Don't type them up for them, the discipline of doing them for themselves begins the process of internalizing the word.

During the next week, suggest that they carry the cards around with them. Whenever they begin to entertain worrisome thoughts, have them take a moment and review the verses. Most important, their job for the week is to memorize the verses. Memorizing them will get the word off the page and into the heart where it can do some good. You might compare this assignment to a doctor who has given a prescription. The patient has read the instructions on the label and thought, "sounds good to me," but failed to take the pills. Just as the prescription is powerless to heal as long as it is in the bottle, the word is impotent to revitalize until it is into the heart. That is why memorization is vital.

Once the verses have been memorized, have your clients develop a ritual by which they can review those verses several times a day. Have them connect the review with something routine. Perhaps every morning in the car before the radio goes on. It might be at meal times, while shaving, walking the dog, or just about anything. The point is to make the verses such an essential part of their thought processes that reviewing them becomes instinctive. Finally, every time a worrisome thought harasses them, they are to begin to quote the verses to themselves one right after another. While they may need to go through them two or three times, the net result will be "taking every thought captive in obedience to Christ." Confronting worrisome thoughts with Scripture and repeating the process of review will produce the fruit of peace within the hearts of your clients and recreate a whole new way of thinking that is healthy rather than toxic.

Getting Set for Session Four

When you finish the third session, the counseling process is more than half over. Hopefully your worriers have been able to experience some success either at understanding the worry process or perhaps curtailing the time spent worrying. With these positive gains, your clients will be prepared to benefit from the final two sessions.

Counselors are wise when they remind counselees at this point that only two sessions remain. This reminder is not aimed at conveying rejection but at reinforcing the limited number of sessions that we informed them about in the first session. Your reminder will help worriers bring in questions and topics for discussion in the final meetings.

Be sure to review the work your counselee is doing for homework. If you are using *Why Worry?*, your clients should be writing down some valuable information in connection with those lessons. If you show some interest in that material, counselees will feel even more clearly that time spent working through those studies is worthwhile.

Our next session's emphasis will be on behavior. In some ways, changing our actual patterns of action is much harder than exploring feelings or cogitating on cognition. Pray for your worrying clients that they will be able to take the steps needed to see long-lasting behavioral change occur.

Be sure to challenge your counselees not to worry about the last two sessions. The normal pattern might include fretting about not having a scheduled session after the fifth visit. But if we have made any progress at all with our clients, facing termination of the counseling process without giving in to worry may be a healthy opportunity to put new feelings, thoughts, and behaviors into practice.

5

Acting on Worry

The Engagement Stage: Session 4

Scripture and the *Behavior* of Worry

A poster displayed in the conference room of a computer manufacturer showed three large hippopotami standing around with their gigantic mouths wide open. The words on the poster read, "When all is said and done, more is said than done." Much of life is like that: everybody has an idea, but rare is the individual who puts his ideas and concepts into action. While much of what's been said thus far implies action, this chapter is devoted to action. This chapter is the "so-what" to what's been said. "So-what's" are important. Without them, we are like the individual described by James 1:24: "Anyone who listens to the word but does not do what it says is like a man who looks at his face in a mirror and, after looking at himself, goes away and immediately forgets what he looks like."

The pivotal passage for us during the previous two chapters has been Philippians 4. In verses six and seven Paul addressed the feelings associated with worry. He claimed that Jesus Christ would stand guard over our feelings if we were willing to take our anxieties to him in prayer. In verse eight Paul discussed the importance of our thoughts. He promised that the God of peace would continue to be with us, protecting our minds from worrisome thoughts if we would carefully screen what we place into our minds. In verse nine, Paul described the final step necessary for us to continue to experience the protective power of the God of peace. Paul wrote, "Whatever you have learned or received or heard from me, or seen in me—put it into practice. And the God of peace will be with you." Paul's three-fold assault upon worry looks like this:

1. Feeling worried? Pray!
2. Thinking worrisome thoughts? Focus upon the things that are good, protect your perspective!
3. Want lasting victory over worry? Practice what you have learned, received, heard, and seen. Paul was saying, "take action."

Paul was an excellent mentor. He had not only taught his followers about the worry-free lifestyle, but he had modeled it too. He referred to what they had "heard" from him and "seen" in him. They had heard and seen an individual who experienced the absence of worry and the peace of God. They had watched Paul pray, as well as to protect his mental input. Now the time had come for the worriers in Philippi to take action.

The third step described by Paul is a crucial one for people who worry. With a couple of strokes of his pen he wrapped up his thoughts on worry with remarkable insight. He used several different words to describe the action necessary to deliver worry it's final death blow. He said, "Whatever you have learned." The word "learned" placed an emphasis upon understanding. It went well beyond learning by rote, and into the arena of learning where one understood principles, as well as the precepts. Paul then used the word "received." That word meant to bring something very near. The word carried overtones of "seizing something for one's own possession." The application for worriers today is that we own the biblical teachings about worry as our very own. Putting the two words together would refer to one who has grown to understand fully the biblical principles, and is ready to apply them personally.

The next step Paul recommended was to "practice" what they had learned and received. The word revolved around the idea of habit. It meant to habitually do something over and over until one was able to experience a desirable level of performance. One interesting twist associated with the word was the idea that one's actions were never really completed. Paul chose this word so that his readers would understand that defeating worry wasn't a one-time event. Habitual worriers will need to practice what they have learned for a lifetime! Although some times will be easier than others, the struggle with worry will always be a threat to their peace of mind.

When our children were little, we often watched them sit behind the wheel of our car and pretend to drive. They would try to turn the wheel, make motor noises, use the signal lights, and sometimes honk the horn. Despite all the effort and time spent behind the wheel, two things didn't happen. First, they weren't going anywhere since they were living in a world of make-believe. Second, make-believe driving didn't make them good drivers. One of our children is fifteen now—need we say more? We can tell you firsthand that watching a four-year-old Jaime pretend to drive a car is really different than riding with a fifteen-year-old Jaime and watching the speedometer push 60 mph! You can bet we have been practicing Paul's three-step prescription for worry! Our point is this: the time has come for your clients to get the car out of the garage and put into practice what they have learned. There comes a time when the best of intentions are simply not enough.

Failing to take action can carry ominous consequences. The book of James is a book of action. Through James, God tells us two things about acting upon what we know. First, James 2:20 says, "You foolish man, do you want evidence that faith without deeds is useless?" His point is obvious. Knowledge must get out of the mind and into application, or it is worthless. Second, James 4:17 says, "Anyone, then, who knows the good he ought to do and doesn't do it, sins." God has always placed a premium upon action, and the arena of worry is no different. When we know what to do and we fail to do it, the Bible labels it "sin." We must abandon worthless speculation and get to the practical application of truth. Unfortunately, failing to act upon our worry often allows the effects of inactivity to snowball so that we actually have more to worry about!

The Scriptures have several specific things to say about worry and action. First of all, we must not allow worry to paralyze us. In Luke 21:34 Jesus said, "Be careful, or your hearts will be weighed down with . . . the anxieties of life." The heart that was "weighed down" was one that was so excessively burdened that it was on overload. That person simply could not function. The "anxieties of life" had proved too stressful for the individual. The word "anxiety" referred to the toxic thinking that resulted in disruption of the personality and the mind. Jesus warned that we must not tolerate that kind of inactivity within our lives.

Jesus illustrated an individual who was paralyzed by worry in Matthew 5. He told the story of a wealthy man who entrusted some of his assets to his servants. The first servant received five talents, the second received two, and the third received one. While the rich man was away the first two servants went into action and through careful investments were able to double their master's money. When their master returned, he commended them for their action and invited them to share in his happiness. However, the third servant failed to act. He simply buried the cash. When his master asked why he hadn't taken action, he answered, "I was afraid." His fear of failure had paralyzed him, so he "went out and hid the talent in the ground." His master rebuked him severely for failing to take action and confiscated the lazy servant's talent. The application is all too clear. Failing to take action displeases the Lord and complicates our lives.

The Scriptures not only tell us to act, but provide us with some excellent guidelines for our action. James 4:13 describes some businessmen who were busy making plans for the future. They were discussing all of their possibilities and trying to plan accordingly. While planning for the future is certainly commendable, living in the future is not. Worriers tend to live in the future. James rebuked them for the endless speculation concerning tomorrow, and corrected their course with the statement, "Why, you do not even know what will happen tomorrow" (James 4:14). When we allow ourselves to worry about the future we consume priceless time and energy churning over the unknown. Worry is like sitting in a rocking chair, it will give you something to do, but it won't get you anywhere. James' focus was upon today. He was encouraging his readers to quit living in the uncertainty of tomorrow and to take action now!

Essentially, Jesus said the very same thing in Matthew 6:34: "Therefore do not worry about tomorrow, for tomorrow will worry about itself. Each day has enough trouble of its own." While Jesus said that we were not to worry about tomorrow, he stressed the concept of living one day at a time. In addition to living one day at a time, Jesus' words seem to imply that worriers should act upon today's troubles, rather than being immobilized today by worrying about tomorrow. Worrying is the interest we pay on tomorrow's problems, and the interest rate is always too high. That is why Jesus said to let tomorrow worry about itself and do what can be done today.

Continuing the Process

Begin your fourth session by reviewing the homework assignments you gave. Encourage your clients to talk. What has been most difficult during the past week? Where did they experience victories? Let them express their frustrations and fears. Those making little progress may be wondering what is wrong with them. Some may be worried about the fact that this is the next to the last session and they haven't made as much progress as they had hoped. The important thing is to listen, affirm their efforts, and convey hope. They didn't become "world-class worriers" in a day, neither will they break lifelong patterns in just a few weeks. Listen for anything they might say that is related to worry and actions. By doing so, you may be able to probe further and apply their situation to some of the Scriptures associated with action.

Following a time of listening, review with your client what you have discovered together during the previous sessions. We have found it very helpful to summarize each session with a word or phrase. It may be different with every client, but we look for an irreducible concept to associate with each session. We as people are very forgetful. We tend to remember less than ten percent three days later of what we have been taught. That is why reviewing the bottom line of each session is very important. We try to summarize our whole process with the phrase: "Faith is the oil in the machinery of life, worry is the sand." I have them repeat it out loud with me. While all this may sound simplistic, your clients will never forget it. From there, review the theme of your first session. The goal was that they simply accept the Bible's categoric condemnation of worry. Put simply, "Worry is wrong." The second session's focus was upon feelings. The phrase that many find memorable is this, "Feelings are fickle." Since feelings are fickle, we need to place a priority on prayer. This might be a good time to ask your clients about their prayer journal, and how prayer is impacting their feelings.

Continue your review with a review of the third session that dealt with thoughts. Here the irreducible concept is "thinking turned toxic." We must guard our perspectives; in doing so we go a long way toward combating the thoughts of worry. Put together, your conversation might sound something like this:

Counselor: "Our summary statement is . . ."
Together: *"Faith is the oil in the machinery of life, worry is the sand."*
Counselor: "Session one?"
Together: *"Worry is wrong."*
Counselor: "Session two?"
Together: *"Feelings are fickle."*
Counselor: "Session three?"
Together: *"Thinking turned toxic."*

We have also found that reviewing the word attached to each of the divine alternatives is a very helpful memory tool. The three key words from the Philippian passage are "prayer," "perspective," and as the focus of today's session, "practice."

Following the assessment of your clients' progress, and after reviewing the principles from previous weeks, work through the Scriptures that focus upon taking action. The goal of all this is to get them to be willing to act. Many people do not act because they do not feel like taking action. They erroneously believe that feelings must precede action. That simply is not true. Our feelings often follow, and are dictated by, our course of action.

Behavior and Worry

Some readers may be surprised that we are dealing with behavior and worry since worry is such a cognitive function. Why not just concentrate on changing the thinking patterns? The answer rests in the fact that the surest way to solidify new understandings about worry is to help the client put new behaviors in place. The behaviors we wish to encourage will be antidotes to the previous patterns.

Changing behavior is difficult. Guatemalan folk traditions contain accounts of worry dolls. Shoppers can still find these six brightly colored dolls in Indian markets in Guatemala. Worriers were to tell each doll one worry before going to sleep and then the doll would work on solving the worry while the owner slept. If such strategies actually worked, changing worry patterns would be much simpler. The fact remains, however, that change is much more difficult than merely talking to a doll or to a pastoral counselor.

The Difficulty of Change

Much of the difficulty in change stems from a fear of social ridicule. For sensitive people, shame and humiliation are tortuous. Many people would prefer the inconvenience of their extensive worry patterns than to risk further the social shaming they often feel is attached to future events. Yet we must convince these worriers that they will benefit from change, even though the changing process might seem uncomfortable. Dr. Paul Hauck expressed the dilemma of the worrier well.

> There is discomfort in changing and there is discomfort in not changing. However, the discomfort connected with changing your behavior or with overcoming your fears has an ending, whereas the annoyance that you have if you don't face your fears can go on until you die (Hauck 1975, 16).

Replacement Behaviors

The following list of three behaviors are strategic because they replace their destructive counterparts with behaviors that will improve the condition of worriers. The pastoral counselor may wish to spend time on these three replacement behaviors during this fourth session.

Action in place of inaction. We have seen how the worry process locks worriers into endless loops of thought that rarely include any action. Because worriers never take any preventive steps that might help lessen the dread, no constructive progress occurs. Worry is a passive activity. We need to help worriers identify actions that will help change their attitudes about the future.

We have already mentioned John Bunyan's character in *Pilgrim's Progress*, Mr. Despondency and his daughter Mrs. Much-Afraid. When the small band of pilgrims attacked and killed the Giant Despair, they all rejoiced and threw a big party. Mr. Ready-to-Halt was encouraged enough by the victory to ask Mrs. Much-Afraid to dance. She agreed and, according to Bunyan, "She answered the music handsomely" (Bunyan 1675, 313). Bunyan speaks here to the need for action and activity as an antidote to worry and fear.

How can the pastoral counselor help worriers become more active? First, we must listen to the particular worries described to us by our counselees. Second, we must watch for parts of the story or steps in the worry process where clients could take some constructive action. Finally, we must challenge counselees to implement these actions and to be accountable to us for carrying the actions out.

If counselees worry about poor performance, we should help them arrange for adequate advance preparation. If counselees worry about feeling and experiencing humiliation, we should help them learn to laugh at themselves when in such situations. If counselees worry about financial reversals, we should help them take steps toward good fiscal planning. If counselees worry about situations where they do not know what to say, we should help them write out possible scripts. The basic principle is simple: watch for behaviors that will help take the energy out of the passive worry process.

Good problem solving in place of poor problem solving. Worriers focus on the first steps of problem solving: defining the problem, identifying options, and exploring possibilities. They do not get beyond this data-gathering stage. They need to learn how not to spend time on relatively minor eventualities, to sort through all the options to identify those that demand attention, to let go of the remaining concerns, to choose the best courses of action, and then to put those solutions into place. At this point in the therapy process counselees should realize that they have spent inordinate amounts of time on very unimportant matters. Most of what we worry about is notoriously unspectacular.

How can we help counselees with this new behavior? You may choose to spell out the standard approach to problem solving (defining the problem, listing alternatives, selecting the best solutions, implementing that solution) for your counselees. Then you could ask them to identify those steps that they have recently focused on in connection with a current set of worries. Finally, counselees may feel the challenge of moving the problem-solving process farther along.

Facing events in place of avoiding them. Avoidance is the expertise most worriers bring to the task of facing the future. With some help from the Holy Spirit we can encourage worriers to embolden themselves and to face matters more directly. We can help with this new behavior if we are able to help counselees identify just what they are avoiding. Very often the issues they are trying to avoid are far less problematic than is the worrying process itself.

As you can readily see, all three of these new replacement behaviors are intertwined. They all interconnect, and the counselee will have difficulty doing one and not the others. But each has a different starting point and may merit individual attention. We should also remember that friends and family members can be allies to us as pastoral counselors. For example, spouses may be very gifted at helping worriers discover actions to take, issues to face directly, and better patterns of problem solving. If we can enlist friends and family in helping our counselee implement these new behaviors, our chances for success greatly increase.

New Action Strategies

During your fourth session together, you will want to review the progress of your clients, to go through the Scriptures relating to the importance of action, and to help your clients learn to develop an action strategy. The hope is that you will be able to assist them by replacing useless worry with productive activity. Sometimes all they can do is pray. Sometimes the need is to take a careful look at the kind of input they have been receiving. Perhaps they have overdosed on society's troubles and need to take personal action to restore balance to their mental input.

Sometimes your clients will be worried about something that could be resolved if they had the courage to act. Fear can be so paralyzing that chronic worriers would rather worry about a given situation than make the phone call to find out if their worry is justified. Some actually worry that their worries might be confirmed! Our intention is to assist them by keeping short accounts on the things about which they worry. We must help them practice being proactive so that every area of unnecessary worry has an objective response. This will counteract your clients' subjective feelings or fears.

When your clients worry, there are five questions that will help them develop an action plan. The first question is pretty basic: "*What are you worried about?*" One of the differences between anxiety and worry is the ability to identify the source of irritation. Someone who is anxious will not be able to define why. When asked, "What's wrong?" an anxious person will often respond with, "I don't know, I just feel like I'm spinning inside." While worry and anxiety are certainly related, it really helps to know if your clients are anxious or worried. If anxiety is the problem, they will not be able to develop an action plan because they can't identify any specifics to act upon. The focus of this entire chapter is virtually useless for anxious individuals.

In contrast to anxious individuals, those who are worried will be able to tell you what they are worrying about and why. Their list might include several things that are troubling them, but a worrier will be able to come up with a specific list. When your client is developing an action plan, it is critical that they deal with one issue at a time. Their action plan shouldn't address thirteen different things at the same time. Most people (if not everyone) who look at a monumental task become discouraged and perhaps give up too soon. It is important that large tasks be broken down into manageable tasks. The chronic worrier may find great difficulty at this point. One of the contributing factors to their worrisome approach to life might rest in their inability to break down large worries into smaller ones. As a result, they have developed a habit of being overwhelmed by the complexity or potential consequences of daily living. Rather than being proactive, they have developed a pattern of being inactive or reactive. The results of inactivity or reactivity have confirmed their worrisome fears. It's a vicious cycle of self-fulfilling prophecies that we as counselors must help our clients reverse.

As they learn to write down what they are worried about, teach them to limit the description to a few words. The shorter the better. You do not want them writing something like this: "I'm worried about Aunt Emma coming to live with us because she is so hard to take care of. She is so grumpy that nobody in the family likes her. However, if I don't take her in, my sister will think I'm a really selfish person. My sister already dislikes me because I didn't come to her Christmas party." The spin can be endless! Adding complexity and detail to the situation will often reinforce worry patterns. If your clients were answering the first question, the best response would be, "I'm worried about Aunt Emma living with us."

The second question is *Would a stranger agree with you?*" The underlying question is concerned with the legitimacy of their worry. All world-class worriers will be able to cite fifty reasons why their worry is legitimate. Would anyone else who is personally removed from the situation agree? Your clients must learn to step out of their subjective world of fear and arrive at an objective perspective. The "yeah-buts" of life tend to melt into insignificance when objectivity and faith are allowed to rule. When explaining this concept to your clients, you might want to play the role of the worrier while they play the role of the stranger. Select a situation that is totally unrelated to your clients, even ridiculous. Perhaps you might want to pretend that you are worried about your car catching fire on Friday the 13th. Be as subjective as possible. Talk about the possibility of fuel lines leaking on a hot engine or the wiring shorting out. Defend your irrational fear with all the "yeah-buts" you can think of. The task of your clients is to play the role of a stranger and to help you see the toxic nature of your worrisome spin. Hopefully, they won't begin to agree with you and start worrying about their car!

Following your 45-second role play, you will want to point out the shallow nature of your "yeah-but" arguments. Sure, the wiring could short out and start a fire, but has it ever happened before? You clients are quite likely to concede that worrying about a burning car on Friday the 13th is rather unfounded. From there, you may decide to address an issue from the worry list of your clients. Play the role of a stranger with them and point out every illogical aspect of their worry. Strip away all of the nonsensical trappings that have been associated with their worry and bring them to the core of the problem, if there is one. They need to learn and instinctively practice playing the role of the stranger upon themselves. After running their personal worry through the grid of a stranger's perspective, all that should remain is a bulletproof case for reasonable worry. Anything less should be viewed as illogical or faithless.

The third question is this: "*What could you do right now?*" By the time your clients have answered the first two questions, they should be left with something relatively tangible. The motivation behind this question is to help them identify what could actually be done to relieve the worry of their heart. You'll want to help them explore as many different options as possible. What could be said to relieve anxiety? What question could be asked? What information is missing that might contribute to their worry? Who could be called? What could be done? In nearly every situation, something can be done to eliminate the unknowns or to prepare for them. However, should your clients come to the conclusion that absolutely nothing can be done, then the best action is prayer. Prayer is being proactive. The knowledge that we have thought through every alternative is emotionally helpful. The hearts and minds of your clients will begin to be at ease because everything humanly possible has been done. The final outcome rests within the hands of a loving Heavenly Father who has a far better perspective than we do.

The fourth question is this: "*Which alternative is best?*" Answering this question requires your clients to work through the options before them and select the finest proactive alternative available. It shouldn't take long to answer the question. Some of the alternatives may be desirable, but impossible. A worried mom can't just climb aboard a plane and fly across the country to check up on her daughter who is away at college. She could, however, call, write a letter, send a fax, mail a personal cassette tape, send a family video, or call a friend who has a child away at college to talk about the situation.

The final question is: *"What will you do?"* After selecting the best alternative, an action plan requires action. Not only do your clients need to determine what will be done, but when and how they will do it. This question needs to be answered with as much specificity as possible. A checklist might prove very helpful. Have your clients list all that needs to be done, along with times or dates. Have them list the things that could go wrong and develop a backup plan. If they practice this approach until it becomes a natural part of their reasoning process they will find a diminishing need for writing out the answers to these questions, and a growing ability to be proactive.

Setting the Stage for the Final Session

We have been working with a time-limited counseling format. In many ways this limit on the number of sessions requires a great deal of discipline to execute. The reasons why counselors have such difficulty enforcing the number of sessions involve many factors. Invariably, when the counseling process has gone well, counselee and counselor alike can find good reasons to continue the process. After all, if some counseling has been helpful, will not more counseling be of even greater benefit?

However, counselors need to stick with the original format. Only in the most unusual of circumstances should counselors set aside the five-session limit. If you do not discipline yourself to work within these boundaries, you will soon lose the benefits that derive from this time-limited model.

Thus in getting ready for the final session we should be prepared to handle a request from the counselee to extend the number of sessions. Clearly and firmly the counselor can affirm the value of sessions held to date, encourage the counselee to continue working hard at implementing what has been learned during the first four sessions, and reiterate the five-session limit.

Ending a productive activity is hard for all of us. Terminating counseling can be a difficult chore for many counselees. We need to help them own the progress they have made as work done by themselves. Their gains have not come because the counselor has done the work for them. God will honor their investment in their own future.

Some counselees will worry, in spite of our attempts to decrease their levels of worry, about how to relate to you after the counseling is over. You have learned a great deal about them during these confidential and private sessions. Perhaps they attend your church and will see you frequently in a parishioner-pastor role. The concern is a legitimate one and you should be prepared to discuss the matter with them in the final session. Counselees can benefit from reassurances that all the material discussed during these sessions will remain inviolate, that you will seek to relate to them just as you would any other parishioner, and that you have successfully carried out these goals with many other church members who have been your counselees in the past.

In preparing for the final session you will also want to be ready to review progress the counselee has made. If you have taken process notes regarding this case, you can review those notes. If you have only your memory to search for signs of growth and development the counselee has gained during these few weeks, make a list of the accomplishments so you can share it with your client during the last session. Our goal has been to decrease the amount of worry in their lives. While some may be disappointed that the problem has not totally disappeared, we must assure them that containing the problem, limiting the time spent worrying, and gaining mastery over the processes that fuel the worry are impressive accomplishments. You may have to remind them that the goal was not perfection; if perfection was required you would not be able to serve as a counselor since you too struggle against worry. But with God's help and blessing, both you and the counselee can learn to replace worry with the peace of God that passes all understanding. Toward that goal we all continue to strive.

6

The Last Word on Worry

The Disengagement Stage: Session 5

Final Thoughts from Scripture on Worry

The most comprehensive passage of Scripture on the subject of worry is contained in Matthew 6. While Matthew was the author, the words were from Jesus Christ himself. He was speaking to a vastly different culture than ours; however, worry knows no cultural or economic boundaries. From the Middle East to Manhattan, worry is as common an ailment as the proverbial common cold. No wonder Jesus addressed the subject with such directness.

In Matthew 6:25–26 Jesus said, "Therefore I tell you, do not worry about your life, what you will eat or drink; or about your body, what you will wear. Is not life more important than food, and the body more important than clothes? Look at the birds of the air; they do not sow or reap or store away in barns, and yet your heavenly Father feeds them. Are you not much more valuable than they?" Once again, the Scriptures portray worry as sin. Not only is what Jesus said important, equally crucial is the way he said it. The phrase "do not worry" is a present imperative in the original language. It implied that his listeners/readers were already in a state of worry, and that worry must be terminated right now!

Following his condemnation of worry, Jesus identified the three major sources of worry confronting his followers. The first was food and drink. Food was serious business for ancient people. We certainly have our share of hungry people in America, but as a whole most of us do not worry about our next meal. The people of Jesus' day often worried (and rightfully so) about tomorrow's food. Sometimes the food just ran out or spoiled! Since there wasn't a grocery store on every corner, they couldn't stop by the local 7-11 on the way to Jericho. While concern over food was certainly a legitimate reason for worry, it was still forbidden by Jesus.

In addition to worrying about food, they had to worry about what they might drink. Israel is a dry land. One could walk for miles without coming across any water. That's why the digging of a well was often the first thing the ancient Israelites would do when they acquired a piece of land. They didn't have indoor plumbing, water faucets, or spring water imported from France. If they did not plan carefully, they could run out of water and find themselves very thirsty, or something worse. The non-negotiable nature of food and water serve to make Jesus' point all the more powerful. If they were not to worry about the basic necessities of life, we certainly shouldn't worry either.

Following his command, he gave them a tangible illustration. He suggested that they look to the birds of the air as an example of worry-free living. There are a couple of implications here. First, the birds had to work for their food; it doesn't rain worms! When God commands us "not to worry" he is not calling us to a life of personal inactivity or irresponsibility. The principle is that God promised to provide, but he chooses to do so through human effort. Getting yourself into action with the faith that God will honor your efforts is a superb alternative to worry. Further, a bird's primary concern is always upon today. They are thoroughly content to live a day at a time. Unlike people, they don't build larger nests or bird barns so they can stockpile food. If they are content to live a day at a time, knowing that their needs will be met, so should we. In addition to that, birds don't tend to overindulge. I've never seen a fat sparrow! They don't overindulge because they have an abundance mental-

ity. They instinctively know that there will be food tomorrow. Jesus'
point was obvious. The birds don't sow, reap, or build barns; they
find no need to overindulge because they are daily cared for by
God. If God takes care of the sparrows, certainly he will take care
of you. So what's the worry?

> Said the robin to the sparrow;
> I should really like to know,
> Why these anxious human beings rush about and worry so.
> Said the sparrow to the robin,
> Friend, I think that it must be,
> They have no heavenly Father such as cares for you and me.

Jesus continued, "And why do you worry about clothes? See how
the lilies of the field grow. They do not labor or spin. Yet I tell you
that not even Solomon in all his splendor was dressed like one of
these. If that is how God clothes the grass of the field, which is here
today and tomorrow is thrown into the fire, will he not much more
clothe you, O you of little faith?" (Matt. 6:28–30). With that, Jesus
turned to another worrisome issue: clothing. It was the spring of
the year and the hillsides were ablaze with red poppies. These poppies were breathtaking when set against the deep green grass on
the rolling hills. It was upon one of these hillsides that Jesus delivered his sermon. He spoke of Solomon. Historically, Solomon was
considered the best-dressed king in Israel's history. Jesus drew
upon this common knowledge and compared Solomon's attire with
the flowers growing in the fields around them. He claimed that all
of Solomon's splendor failed to compare with the glory of the flowers. Despite their beauty, the very same flowers were often pulled
up by the roots and used to start fires for cooking. Jesus was
endeavoring to point out the abundance of God's provision. Since
God bothers to clothe the hillsides with beautiful flowers, that are
here today and kindling tomorrow, why then would he not provide
clothing for you?

Remember, Jesus was not talking about the kind of person who
stands in front of a closet full of clothing and complains about not
having a thing to wear. His listeners didn't have much; they were
lucky to have more than one shirt. If something happened to it, it

wasn't easily replaced in a day. It was to that kind of individual that he said, "Don't worry." If they were not to worry, certainly we shouldn't either!

In addition to people worrying about food and fashion, Jesus identified a third worrisome subject: health. In verse 27 Jesus said, "Who of you by worrying can add a single hour to his life?" Many people worry about their health. When *Industry Week* questioned America's managers about personal areas of worry, 74 percent of them identified health and fitness as their number one worry. While worry can't add a single hour to your life, worry can certainly take an hour away. The Mayo Clinic claims that 80–85 percent of their caseload is illness due to mental stress. Worry is the fuel line for stress. At the beginning of the century, bacteria was considered to be responsible for most disease. Today, mental stress is gaining an everincreasing share of the responsibility for people getting sick. Consider this, you can never worry yourself to life, but you can certainly worry yourself to death. When you begin to worry, the hypothalamus in the brain sounds an alarm. The motor area of the brain sends a message to your muscles causing them to tense up. Your nervous system bolsters your muscles for readiness and your heart begins to beat faster. The tiny blood vessels in your stomach shut off the blood supply to your digestive system. Your breathing becomes quicker and more shallow. The stomach muscles and intestines may go into spasms causing that nauseating feeling. Your blood pressure increases and red blood cells are pumped in from the spleen. Your sweat glands open and your saliva dries up. Sugar pours into your system from the liver. To top it all off, the adrenalin gland releases adrenalin into the blood to maintain all of the reactions. A doctor from Johns Hopkins said, "We don't know why it is, but worriers die sooner than nonworriers; that is a fact." No wonder Jesus told his followers not to worry about their lives, it simply isn't healthy!

Jesus concluded his advice on worry with these words, "So do not worry, saying, 'What shall we eat?' or 'What shall we drink?' or 'What shall we wear?' For the pagans run after all these things, and your heavenly Father knows that you need them. But seek first his kingdom and his righteousness, and all these things will be given to you as well. Therefore do not worry about tomorrow, for tomorrow will worry about itself. Each day has enough trouble of its own" (Matt. 6:31–34). These verses contain Jesus' second and third prohibition of worry. However, the second and third command are different from the first. You may remember that the first command was in a Greek tense that said, "Stop worrying, right now." The implication was that he was speaking to people who were worriers. Following his command to stop worrying, he identified the three common areas of their worry: food, fashion, and fitness. Then Jesus told them again, "Do not worry." However, the second and third time he used the ingressive aorist that carried the sense of, "Do not start worrying." When one puts the two concepts together, Jesus said, "Stop worrying right now and don't start worrying again."

There were two additional reasons for refusing to worry. First, "the pagans run after all these things." The characteristic which most clearly identifies godless people is their worrisome pursuit of food, fashion, and fitness. They are utterly absorbed with the quest for security. Since we are people of faith, why should we carry on as if we were faithless pagans? Instead, Jesus said we ought to expend our energy upon the pursuit of eternal things. Perhaps the greatest deterrent to worry is the consistent investment of ourselves in the things that have eternal value. That is why Jesus included, "But seek first his kingdom and his righteousness, and all these things will be given to you as well." The relentless pursuit of the kingdom of God and his righteousness counteracts the worrisome spirit within us and guarantees God's provision for our needs. Psalm 34:10 states it like this, "The lions may grow weak and hungry, but those who seek the LORD lack no good thing."

The second reason for Jesus' prohibition of worry was due to our heavenly Father's knowledge of our basic needs. God understands. He knows that we require food and clothing. He understands our health concerns. As heavenly Father, he knows and promises to provide! Since he has consistently demonstrated his ability to provide for the sparrow and the hillsides, why would he fail to provide for you?

Believing and trusting in God's ability to meet every need is the ultimate goal of worry-free living. Philippians 4:19 says, "And my God will meet all your needs according to his glorious riches in

Christ Jesus." If that's true, why should we worry and fret? That verse is absolutely delightful as well as remarkable. It identifies the source of our provision as "God." It distinguishes the scope of our provision as "all," and it depicts the supply of our provision as "according to *his* riches!" I can't think of a single need that isn't covered by that divine promise. However, I can think of some areas of greed that may be excluded. We often confuse "needs" with "greed." When we do, we start to worry. That is why seeking God's kingdom first is so vital. As we focus upon the eternal, the line between greed and need becomes quite clear to us and our hearts can begin to relax.

Looking Back

During the final session with your client you'll want to review several things. First, you should review your client's progress. Discuss the ups and downs of the previous week. Ask them to identify their greatest challenge and their most significant victory. Focus upon improvement and point out the positive!

Second, take some time to review their prayer list. No doubt there have been some answers to prayer during the past several weeks. Be sure to point out and celebrate those answers. You might want to pause and pray together, thanking the Lord for his gracious provision.

Following prayer, take a quick review of the key phrases and words that were described in chapter five under the heading "Continuing the Process." In addition to what is there, be sure to identify the third "P" in Paul's antidote for worry. The first was "Prayer," the second was "Perspective," and the third was "Practice."

After the overview of your previous sessions together, take ten minutes to review the skills you have imparted to your client. You may want to have your client walk you through the five questions from session four. Have them teach them to you, as if you had never heard them before. Then you might suggest that they tell you how to apply those questions specifically to one of their worrisome problems. You might ask them to identify their most meaningful verse from your study together. Have them describe for you the process of captivating their thoughts and making them obedient to Christ.

Which verses did they memorize and how has the process helped them reprogram their thought life?

One of your concluding exercises should include a guided tour through Matthew 6. Use the passage as a summary of the Bible's perspective on worry. Ask your client if there are any similarities between Matthew 6 and some of the other verses they have studied. Help them to see the stark cultural differences between our world and the world of Jesus. While his followers had every legitimate reason for worry, it was still forbidden by Jesus.

Before you conclude your time together, it is important that your client is able to chronicle change. The best way for one to see change is to put it down on paper. You might find it useful to have your client's final assignment be a diary containing the month's victories. While this is your last session together, you will both be able to celebrate the victories if they mail you a copy. You could respond with a note, phone call, or a simple pat on the back.

You will also want to remind them that what you have endeavored to impart to them are tools. Tools are useless unless they are used. Furthermore, they are only as useful as the skill of the one using them. They will need to continue to practice the principles they have learned on a regular basis. This will insure their growth as human beings, and enable them to continue to refine their faith-filled, worry-free lives.

Finally, remind them of the importance of focus. Beginning with the right focus or intentions does not guarantee that one will continue to do so. Peter is an excellent illustration of one who started out right, but soon found himself literally in over his head! Peter was rowing a small boat on the Sea of Galilee. He and the other disciples were terrified by a terrible storm. They were worried that death was imminent. The disciples certainly had good reason to worry, many had drown in such storms before. From out of the darkness, Jesus came walking to them upon the water. Since the odds for survival did not rest within the boat, Peter stepped out of the boat and onto the water with Jesus. His eyes were fixed upon his Lord. The result was Peter overcoming his fear and walking on the water! Matthew 14:30 states, "But when he saw the wind, he was afraid and began to sink." Once Peter's eyes shifted from the Lord and back to his circumstances, his heart was filled with fear and he began to sink. We often start out courageous enough, but sometimes our circumstances are overwhelming. When our focus begins to drift, we begin to sink. Worrisome thoughts wash over our hearts and minds, and we begin to feel like we are drowning. When (not if) that occurs, follow Peter's example when he cried out, "Lord, save me!" Encourage your client to shift focus back upon our gracious Lord. God isn't angry when we fail. We need not run from him in humiliation; rather, we need to run to him as our source of salvation, strength, and shelter. Just as Jesus reached out his hand in response to Peter's cry for help, he will always be available to stabilize the fleeting heart of your client.

Looking Ahead

Any course of counseling will have some unfinished business. In five sessions with our worriers, we cannot do all that could be done. As pastoral counselors, we must be able to accept what God has allowed us to accomplish and to forgo what we have been unable to do. In most cases these matters do not concern the counselees. However, if we have been unable to address some central issue, we may need to review that omission with clients. For example, "We haven't been able to explore how your worry patterns compare to your family of origin. You may want to give that some attention in the future because such awareness could help you understand more fully your own involvements with worry."

We want our worriers to leave the counseling process with four new tools useful for combating worry. In many ways the following list of four merely summarizes all that we have tried to accomplish through the counseling to date.

Identifying Vulnerability

All worriers will have some unique features to their worry patterns. Some will worry in the face of certain types of stress. Others will worry especially regarding vocational or job-related matters. Yet others may struggle most intensely with worry when they are tired or worn down by overwork and fatigue. In each case worriers need to understand their own patterns of, and vulnerabilities to, worry.

If counseling has done anything for our worriers, the process should have taught them to be particularly diligent in putting new-found skills into place at moments of highest vulnerability. For example, if counselees know that the time for their annual pay raise review at work is a peak worry time, they can anticipate this tendency to increase worry at that time by taking proactive steps. Perhaps participating in a discipling relationship that includes accountability for this particular problem may be a helpful strategy. Or counselees could recontact you as a pastoral counselor for a single review session at the very time of highest vulnerability. We do not want clients to leave counseling with the thought, "If my worry pattern ever returns, I am a failure at counseling and I will never reach out for help again." We want our counselees to be better prepared for some future reoccurrence of the struggle.

Self-Monitoring

Another major benefit of counseling consists of the increased awareness the counselee now has of internal processes. The inner life of most people remains puzzling and unexplored until they engage in some experience such as counseling. Once people become acquainted with their inner world in a way that gives some mastery or control, they will never be the same. This new awareness is a positive enhancement that generally will be a permanent ability.

We want our counselees to leave the counseling process with this new ability for monitoring the self well in place. We have focused on worry, how to control it, and how to replace it with peace that only God can give. In spite of this focus on worry, we also hope that some of these new skills will spill over into other areas. If our counselees have seen some success in tackling worry, they may experience higher levels of self-confidence when new or different problems occur. The ability to monitor their internal world is a skill that will transfer to other problems our counselees may later face.

New Coping Strategies

We have tried to expose our worrying clients to new coping strategies regarding the feelings of worry, the cognitions of worry, and the behavior of worry. Perhaps our counselees have responded more to one of these areas than to others. But we do hope that they can leave counseling with several of these new coping strategies in active use. We must be careful to remind our counselees that in some instances matters may seem worse while they are getting better. A surgeon often gives a preoperative patient the same message. "Your surgery tomorrow will correct some long-term problems. In the long run you will feel better even though your discomfort for a few days immediately after the operation may make you wonder if the operation was worthwhile." Sometimes counselors must give counselees that same perspective.

We also want our counselees to know that the return of intense worry on some future occasion does not indicate the total failure of counseling. Instead, such an eventuality simply gives our clients a challenging opportunity to utilize all the new coping strategies that they have learned while in counseling.

Christ as Companion

We have discovered that the Bible says a great deal about worry. Worry is not God's ideal for the believer; peace is that ideal. The peace of God is his unique provision to the worrier. Where peace reigns, worry is quiescent. Our hope for the counselee is that these truths can serve as a solid foundation for an integrated conquest of worry. We have aimed at building a healing process for the worrier that addresses spiritual, psychological, and interpersonal issues. The truths from God's word about peace form the basis for recovery from worry.

As a parting emphasis, we need to remind the counselee that Christ is a companion during times of worry and times of peace. Jesus promised his followers that he would never leave them nor forsake them. He promised that he is with us until the end of the age. These statements of Jesus are cogent to the dilemmas of the worrier. Whereas the worrier feels fearful, vulnerable, and threatened by the future, the everpresent Jesus is, in fact, with the believer even in the midst of those difficult times. The crucial question is not, "Is Jesus a companion to the worrier?"; the critical question is, "Does the worrier realize that Jesus is a companion in the midst of the worry?"

We are not alone in our struggles. God has not abandoned us to the terrors of uncertainty. Yet God does not force himself on us; we must acknowledge his presence by faith and learn to rely on that knowledge as our help in the time of trouble.

So when our counselees come ready to graduate from our brief counseling series of sessions, we are not sending them out alone into an uncertain future. One of our greatest contributions to them can be to send them forth with renewed confidence in Jesus their companion, no matter what the future may hold.

Referrals

You may have discovered that your worrying counselee has profited to some degree from the five sessions of counseling, but has, in fact, great emotional needs beyond what you are equipped to handle. How do you ascertain that your counselee needs more help? The following criteria illustrate some of the conditions that would merit referral.

1. If your counselee has been unable to accomplish the simplest of homework tasks because of extensive anxiety and distraction.
2. If you have found that in addition to worry your counselee struggles with agoraphobia (fear of being in places or situations from which escape is difficult) or a panic disorder (periods of intense fear).
3. If you have discovered that the client is suicidal or psychotic (out of touch with reality).
4. If your client is the victim of severe abuse or trauma and has not yet received any professional help.
5. If your client struggles with a substance use or abuse disorder (alcohol or illegal drugs, for example).

Should you discover such a need for referral you must remember that your five session counseling program may have served some very important and strategic goals. Your counseling may prove to be a helpful prelude to further help that others can provide. Perhaps your counselee initially revealed just a portion of her or his struggles just to "test the waters." Your help could calm understandable fears and help pave the way for future needed help.

To whom do you refer? This question raises larger issues that relate to all of your pastoral work. In the course of other pastoral care activities you will encounter people in need of professional help in addition to your counseling.

First we should briefly discuss the advice that some authors give to pastors: Refer your church members *only* to counselors who *only* use the Bible for their counseling. This advice may be well-intentioned but you are ill-advised if you seek to follow this philosophy rigidly. The reason is quite simple: all mental illness is not the result of personal sin. The spiritual responsibilities we have to confess our sins, repent, accept God's forgiveness, and move on with life are vital tasks for all of us. But these spiritual tasks deal with sin. They do not deal with the damage done to us by the sins of others, they do not deal with emotional illnesses that have genetic or biological involvements, and they do not deal with psychological handicaps that originate in the early development of the personality. Those who teach that believers never need psychological help from trained professionals must squint at the data, ignore the obvious, and distort reality to make the distress of parishioners fit their paradigm.

Nonetheless you will want to refer to trained professionals who themselves are believers and who are committed both to the emotional and spiritual well-being of their clients. Christian therapists now serve most all metropolitan areas of the United States. If you are in a region, however, where your parishioners cannot travel to see a believing therapist, you will need to seek out a competent psychotherapist who may or may not share your church's exact set of beliefs. Currently, professional standards of competence for all therapists include the duty to respect the individual's ethnic and religious traditions. Thus, competent therapists, even though they may be secular and unbelieving, are supposed to respect the religious beliefs of their clients. But because not all therapists conduct their practices in accord with this level of competence, you should personally know those to whom you refer.

Most therapists will be glad to meet you for lunch so that the two of you can lay the groundwork for a mutually beneficial relationship. Obviously you may not be able to arrange these visits at the last minute, but in time you can develop a knowledge of available therapists so that you are prepared when the time to refer arrives. The key ingredient to look for among otherwise well-trained professionals is a commitment to respect the religious convictions of clients.

How do you address the need for referral with counselees? The answer to this difficult issue will vary greatly with the personality of your counselee, your level of rapport with that counselee, and how much you have discussed this type of issue before the fifth and final session. None of us responds well to shock or surprise. We have to initiate a discussion of referral with sensitivity and care. Counselees need to know that your recommendations for referral for further help are based on your concerns for their best welfare and are not an expression of abandonment or rejection. You should state your reasons for making the referral in terms counselees can well understand. Avoid technical jargon or diagnostic labels. Couch your comments in a confident reassurance that help is available and that they can profit by addressing these remaining issues. Be sure to ask counselees for their reactions to your recommendations. Their responses will help you correct misimpressions or misunderstandings.

Ideally you will want to give clients a choice of names. You may feel that you do not have that luxury and can only give one referral name. In any event, be sure to explain how to call for an appointment. If possible and with your counselee's permission, try to call the therapist the counselee selects to give the therapist your reasons for the referral. Often a therapist will appreciate the interest shown by a pastor in the ongoing welfare of a new client. The therapist may even be open to coordinating ongoing care so that you can continue to provide supportive pastoral oversight while the professional therapy is in progress.

Good referrals, well-made to competent therapists, can greatly enhance our ministry to those in need. Be sure to follow up on your suggestions so as to provide the additional encouragement that might be needed for the counselee to seek the help that is needed.

The End

As their pastor, you will have both informal and formal contact in the days ahead. Formal contact will occur every Sunday as you deliver your message. Informal contact could occur anywhere from the hardware store to the church picnic. You'll want them to understand that every time you see them you won't be wondering about the worry in their lives. While you are certainly concerned, counselees sometimes interpret words from the pulpit as a direct reference to them or their situation. While you would never do that, people tend to hear our words through their own mind-set and have an uncanny ability to draw inaccurate conclusions. Moreover, a passing comment at the church door might be taken as having special overtones for them and their struggle with worry. When this occurs, no doubt your previous client has vastly overestimated the importance of their worry in your life and mind. Nevertheless, we always tell counselees that we hear so much personal information in any given month that we certainly will not be remembering the specifics of their struggles and viewing them, either formally or informally, as worrisome individuals. They need to know that they have not been labeled by you, and anything that tends to confirm their fears of being labeled is simply miscommunication.

Saying goodbye can be difficult. At the conclusion of your five weeks together, some will feel a bit apprehensive about being cut loose from your pastoral support. You might want to reassure them that they will continue to be in your thoughts and prayers. Convey to them your excitement about the coming months ahead since they will undoubtedly grow in their faith. People need someone to believe in them. You can be the individual who affirms them by your words of confidence. Let them know that there will be difficult times ahead, but reassure them that they have the tools to confront every worrisome situation. Your concluding role with your clients is that of a cheerleader who believes in them!

In terms of future contact and follow-up, you may include a checkup call or card to your previous client. You might flip through your calendar and mark a date three months from now so you'll remember to give them a quick phone call or send them a short note. You might ask them to mail you a copy of their prayer journal in a month or two. While no pastor is looking for more work, we have found that we can often respond personally to people's correspondence by writing a short note (ten or fifteen words) right on their letter with a brightly colored pen and mailing it back to them. It doesn't take much time, but it tells them that their letter made it to your desk and that you care enough to read it and respond. I've found that people appreciate the personal touch of a handwritten note from someone as busy as their pastor.

How has the counseling process you have just completed affected you? We are not disconnected from our ministry activities. What we do with and for people has an impact on our lives as well. We minister best when we allow our ministry to others make its impact on our own lives as well.

Have you discovered in the course of working with your worrier that you worry quite a bit yourself? Perhaps you never realized that your levels of worry actually represent a problem you should address in your own life. Could God be speaking to you as well to combat this insidious problem with some of the new perspectives and coping strategies that you have just taught your client? If so, don't miss out on this valuable challenge to grow in faith and to develop your Christlikeness.

7

A Case History
of a World-Class Worrier

Session One

I wouldn't say that I was worried about finding a "world-class worrier," but I've got to admit that I was a bit concerned. Given the time frame available to me, I wondered if I would be able to find someone who would qualify as a "world-class worrier." My first session with Allison relieved me of all my worries, I mean, "concerns."

Allison is in her late thirties and has been married for 18 years. She and her husband have had some bumpy times together, but they are basically a happily married couple and blessed with healthy children. Allison and her husband are middle-class people. Both of them need to work in order to make ends meet. Like most Americans, they often run out of money before they run out of month. Much of Allison's worries center on the issue of personal finance.

I explained to Allison that we would be meeting together for a maximum of five sessions. I also explained that there would be homework involved and asked if she would be willing to complete it. She agreed to do the assignments and added that she would be willing to do anything necessary to relieve her chronic worry. As it turned out, Allison was very eager to receive help. As we talked through the related Scriptures, she enthusiastically jotted down some notes.

I asked Allison to rate her level of worry. "Allison," I said, "on a scale of one to ten how would you . . . " Before I could finish the question, she responded, "9.75." I said, "Are you telling me that it would be nearly impossible for you to worry more than you do now?" She responded with an emphatic, "I can't think of many things I don't worry about." I responded with a smile and said, "Come on, isn't there something you don't worry about?" She rolled her eyes, thought for a moment and said, "Nothing comes to mind." With that, she laid to rest my concerns of finding a world-class worrier.

As I began to take an inventory of Allison's worry, it was apparent that she had been worrying for a long time. Her skills had been honed and polished for many years. She described her childhood days as ones filled with anxiety. Her mother was what she called "a stage mother" in that Allison was taken from audition to audition trying out for various parts in plays and musicals. The cycle was endless. Allison was constantly under pressure to perform and get a part. Early on, she developed painful habits associated with the fear that she might not measure up. By high school, worry had become commonplace. She stated that she would try out for parts in musicals and then spend sleepless nights second-guessing herself and her performance. She was plagued by the "If only's" in her life. She would rerun the audition over and over again in her mind, wondering if she had done as well as she could have. She said that she would pray and try to make deals with God. Her deals often consisted of things like, "God, if you get me this part, I promise I'll . . . " By her teenage years, she had placed expectations upon herself that were far beyond reality. The growing difference between her expectations and her performance was a constant agitating source of worry.

Much of what Allison talked about revolved around failing to fulfill the expectations of others. She indicated that a fear of failure had established patterns of worry early in life. Later, those same patterns had spilled over into every other arena of life. Not only did Allison worry about her life and everything attached to it, but worry for others consumed her. She constantly worried on behalf of her friends and family. For example, a friend of hers is going through a rather ugly divorce. Her friend is a Christian and seems to be facing the uncertainty of her future with a great deal of courage and confidence. This worries Allison. She worries that her friend doesn't worry enough. Allison not only worries about herself and the worries of others, she worries that other people don't worry!

I pressed her for some specifics from her own life. She insisted that she worried about everything, but I asked for some specific examples. She identified three specific areas of worry that continually plague her life. The first area was alluded to earlier. She frequently worries about what other people will think of her. "Was I good enough? Am I nice enough? Could I have done it better? I wish I could do that again." At every turn of life, Allison questions the fact that she has done all she could, and should have done.

The second area of worry revolves around the issue of money. Money has been a long-standing problem within the family. While both Allison and her husband are employed, like many Americans, they live from paycheck to paycheck. She wonders if they'll ever really get ahead. Although they have been married for nearly twenty years, they have yet to purchase their own home. She worries about the future, a college education for her children, retirement, and dozens of other things. Since there is rarely a reserve, she plays the "What if" game. "What if my husband gets hurt . . . ? What if I lose my job? What if . . . ? What if . . . ?"

The third area of worry revolves around her health. Allison worries about every virus that comes along. She's sure that she'll catch it. Sometimes she makes herself sick worrying about getting sick. When I asked her why the excessive worry over health, she looked at me and said, "Because both my mom and dad died of cancer."

Today was indeed a good day for us to begin our first session. Two days ago, Allison discovered a lump in her breast. True to form, her heart began to play the "What if . . . ?" game with more fervency than ever. "What if it's cancer? What if I lose my breast? What if I die? Who will take care of my children? What will happen to my husband?" The list of "What if's . . . ? " was certainly endless.

Interestingly enough, she did indicate receiving a great deal of peace after calling a girlfriend and praying over the phone.

To conclude our inventory on worry, I asked Allison, "When it is all said and done, and the facts are in, how much of your worry do you find justified?" She thought for a moment, and said, "Five percent. It seems to always work out in the end, but as soon as things work out, I put them behind me and I begin to look into the future for something else to worry about." I was hoping at this point Allison would see the futility of worrying. Without a moment's hesitation she understood the concept, and said, "In my mind, I know that everything will be okay. The problem is convincing my heart."

Following the inventory on worry, I asked Allison to visualize five stair steps that I would like for her to climb in her mind. The first step was labeled "*Faith*." This step was meant to remind her that everyone lives every day by faith in something. I illustrated some of the areas where she exercises faith on a daily basis. From applying the brakes on a car, to eating canned food, to balancing her accounts at the end of the day, most things we do require faith. Having understood that, we took the next step.

The second step she was to visualize was labeled "*Faith in God*." My hope was that she would see the inconsistency of exercising daily faith in a hundred different things and yet her inability to place faith in the Almighty God. Within just a few moments she grasped the concept and said, "It is ironic that I can have faith in my Ford, but not faith in my heavenly Father." "Ironic, indeed!" I added. At this point, I said, "Allison, there's a phrase that we're going to use in our sessions together." The phrase goes like this, "Faith is the oil in the machinery of life, worry is the sand." Having a husband who is a mechanic and into cars and boats, she was able to visualize the analogy. I told her that faith will give her the ability to move smoothly through life, while worry will simply wear her out.

Having reviewed the first two steps once again, I asked Allison to visualize a third step in our five-step thought process. The third step was labeled "*Worry is wrong*." It was here that we read the biblical injunctions against worry. We read together from Matthew 6 and Hebrews 11:6. I encouraged Allison to buy into the idea that worry is wrong. We talked through some of the key issues described in chapter two of this book as they pertained to Hebrews 11 and

Matthew 6. Since Allison did not seem to be guilt laden, I asked her to describe God's feelings about worry. She clearly and concisely explained that worry was wrong. In no way did she endeavor to justify her own personal worry; rather, she expressed the hope that she would be able to eliminate it from her life.

With that realization, I asked her to visualize a fourth step. The fourth step is labeled "*God will help you.*" We read through Isaiah 41:10. She had already committed the verse to memory. It seems that when she discovered the lump in her breast, her girlfriend had read that verse to her over the phone before they prayed. Since then, she had reviewed the verse time and time again. I drew her attention to the fact that God was indeed helping her in a miraculous way. She was already coping with the unknown of a lump in her breast. It was a perfect forecast of what God wanted to do in every area of her life. She smiled and responded with, "Then there's hope." "Exactly," I said.

That's the fifth step I wanted her to visualize. Label the fifth step "*Hope.*" As we read through Isaiah 41, I explained to her the meaning of some of the words. She found great comfort in the meaning of the word "dismayed." I told her that the Hebrew word, *Shaah,* meant literally "to gaze." I described it as one who looked at circumstances with amazement or bewilderment. I said, "It is that idea of being paralyzed by fear, and feeling helpless." Her response was interesting. Allison told me that feeling paralyzed was precisely the feeling associated with her worry. She found a lot of consolation in the fact that God understood her feelings and was willing to reinforce and help her. She also found immense comfort in the concept that the word "help" meant to surround. The idea that God promised to wrap his arms around her and sustain her combatted Allison's feelings of bewilderment and helplessness. For whatever reason, probably the uncertainty of her biopsy, this verse really connected with Allison's heart.

We reviewed the stair step visualization once again, and at each step talked about "faith being the oil in the machinery of life." Following the review, I gave Allison the assignment found in chapter two. I handed her a sheet of paper with the seven passages of Scriptures and five questions from the same chapter. I talked through each of the questions so she would understand their primary purpose. I also explained that she should be able to do the assignment in about 15 minutes. Even though the assignment looked excessive, it really wouldn't require a great deal of time. She agreed to have the assignment completed within a week.

Lastly, I took a sheet of paper and divided it in half. I labeled the left half, "*Things to Pray About*," and the right half, "*God's Answers to Things*." I explained that she needed to keep a prayer list of anything and everything that she worries about during the week. Then as God answers her prayers, so that worrisome subjects are no longer worries, she was to write God's answer on the right-hand side of the paper. I suggested that each evening she should conclude her day by praying through the list. In effect, she would be passing her list on to her heavenly Father. While she might likely take up those worries for herself the following day, I explained that prayer would be a crucial ingredient in defeating the worry in her life.

We set the dates for our next sessions together and closed with prayer. I prayed that the next four sessions would be immensely profitable for Allison. I also prayed for her physical condition. I asked the Lord to grant her both peace of mind and a benign report.

Session Two

When Allison entered my office for our second session together, there was a big smile on her face. I assumed that this must have meant good news about the biopsy. After the typical small talk, I asked her about the lump in her breast. She claimed that her prayer had been answered and that everything was okay. I breathed a sigh of relief and said, "That's great, Allison!" She went on to tell me that when the doctor said that it was nothing, she had actually said aloud, "Well, that's an answer to prayer."

I asked Allison what thoughts went through her mind when the lump turned out to be nothing. I was hoping that she would draw the logical conclusion, that her worry had been in vain. She laughed and said, "I immediately began to worry about how much the doctor visit would cost!" I said, "Wait a minute, you just got the most wonderful answer to prayer that you could have ever imagined, and without so much as a blink, you found something new to worry about?" Her answer was classic, "Yea, kind of sick isn't it?"

Finances were always a concern for her and her husband. No sooner had the good news graced her ears than she began to worry about paying for it. She was afraid that she might have to scrape together the 80 or 90 dollars for the doctor visit. When the doctor asked her about her insurance coverage, she told him that it had been cancelled. Graciously, he said, "Well then, how about ten dollars?" I knew we were making progress when Allison responded, "I was worried about the lump, and it was okay; then I was worried about paying for it, and that was okay, too. I suppose God is trying to teach me something."

I asked Allison how she felt about the verses she had read the previous week. She said the most difficult part was knowing in her mind what was right, and yet having her feelings refuse to cooperate. She stated that the previous night she had been worried about something, and yet couldn't identify what it was. This left her very frustrated. I told her that worry is typically identifiable. When you can't identify the source of the worry, the problem is more likely anxiety, which is a more complex issue. I suggested that if she continued to have trouble identifying the source of her worry we might need to take a new approach.

With that she went on to say that most of her feelings revolved around guilt. As she had read the verses and answered the questions, she had become very convicted about worry. She found it hard to accept the fact that her feelings just didn't seem to follow her thinking.

Of all the verses she read, I asked which one had been her favorite. She responded with Matthew 13. As you may remember, that was the parable of the sower. Her comment was that she had been allowing the good soil to be eroded away by worry. As a result, God wasn't able to reproduce within her all that he was capable of producing.

When I asked which passage of Scripture had been most troubling, she responded with the story of the Centurion. "Here is a guy who had so much faith that he could say to Jesus, 'Just say the word and I know my servant will be made well.' How could he say that?" she asked. Allison then raised her hand, and with a sheepish look asked the question, "Could I have an injection of that kind of faith? I mean, here is a guy who isn't even a Christian, and he's got more faith than I'll ever have." It seemed that Allison was beginning to get the picture that faith was indeed "the oil in the machinery of life."

I asked her to summarize what she was feeling in regards to her worry. "It seems to come down to an issue of who is in charge here. I have no problem trusting the Lord for my salvation. I know I can't do anything to win that. But I somehow feel that God may not be concerned about all the details of life that concern me. I guess you could call it selective belief. I have a difficult time with that. Maybe I feel like I have to try harder so I can measure up. That way, God will know I'm sincere and relieve my worry." Allison was still trying to gain approval.

We talked through Jeremiah 17, and identified the deceitful human heart as the culprit behind worry. Allison seemed to find great comfort in another verse that talked about the human heart. First John 3:19 says, "We set our hearts at rest in his presence." It helped her to see that a restless, worrisome heart can be placed at ease. The next phrase explains why: "For God is greater than our hearts." You may remember that one of the major goals for this session is for our counselee to feel hope. I believe that with this verse Allison began to feel hope, perhaps for the first time in a long time.

The final passage that we worked through together was Philippians 4:6–7. While she was familiar with the verses, it was a straightforward reminder that worry is forbidden and prayer is commanded. She really liked 1 Peter 5:7, which states that she could cast all of her anxieties upon him because he cared for her—even the little things in her life. Hope and comfort began to grow when I explained to her that the word "cares" was in a tense that means God never stops caring. Since God never stops caring, we can stop worrying.

We wrapped up our time together with the concluding thoughts from Philippians, which state that the peace of God will guard her heart and mind in Christ Jesus. I explained that the word "guard" described a sentinel on the wall whose job was to scan the horizon for the enemy. Once an enemy was spotted, the sentinel warned the city and then switched roles to that of a warrior. I explained that when she takes her worries to the Lord in prayer, he stands guard over her heart. As a sentinel, he is watching her heart for signs of worry. When the heart begins to worry he alerts the mind, which should prompt us to prayer. Our prayer then enables him to go to war with our treacherous, worrying hearts. It's a beautiful cycle of prayer and protection. For some reason that imagery really connected with Allison. Hope was growing. An awareness of God's undying concern was emerging. Allison felt as though she had an ally in Jesus Christ, not just for salvation, but for winning her personal war with worry.

We closed our second session by praying together and giving her assignments, which concentrated mostly upon her prayer journal.

Session Three

I began our third session by asking Allison how her week had unfolded. She said, "I had the most rotten, horrible, blowout of a weekend!" She then qualified her statement with this, "But it did make me ace my drama audition." While she had experienced a pretty bad weekend in terms of her battle with worry, she was able to recognize progress in terms of her actions. Despite a "horrible, blowout of a weekend," this was progress.

I asked if her week had been any better than her weekend. Her response was that it had been better, but the weekend had really shaken her. She said, "Not only did I worry, but I knew how wrong my worry was, so I felt even more guilty." After further discussion about the weekend, she concluded, "God is really dealing with me. The reason the weekend seemed so bad was because I'm coming to grips with my worry. I'm not going to allow it to immobilize me."

I asked Allison about the highlight of her week. She concluded that her personal discovery of 1 John 5:14 had impacted her the most. The verse says, "This is the confidence we have in approaching God: that if we ask anything according to his will, he hears us." She described to me the nature of her prayer life during the previous week. She found encouragement in 1 John 5, knowing that God heard her prayers and was in the process of answering them. Since the previous week's session had focused upon feelings, I asked her if her feelings of worry had begun to change. "Slightly," she responded. This past week certainly didn't bring the kind of progress I had witnessed the previous week. Allison was reeling from what she considered a major setback.

I asked about her prayer journal. I was a little disappointed that the pages didn't include very many different items or issues. It still focused upon her major worries of performance, money, and health. I had hoped to see more little issues addressed so that she could see progress more readily. I asked if she had seen any specific answer to prayer; she said that she had. She had prayed about a situation involving her husband. There is a man within the community whom he had befriended on a number of occasions. Despite his gestures of friendship, the individual had failed to reciprocate anything in return. Apparently, this individual was a very important person to both of them. That served to intensify the potential for worry. During the week, Allison had been able to take that situation to the Lord in prayer, actually left it with him, and hadn't taken it back. I identified this as great progress! I reviewed the scenario for her so she could see it as a whole. I said, "Allison, here is a significant person in your lives who is suddenly responding inappropriately and callously to your friendship, yet you have been able to overcome your worry. That's great progress!" As she began to see the big picture, I saw a glimmer of hope once again in her eyes. It had suddenly dawned upon her that in the midst of a "horrible, blowout of a weekend," she had actually gained victory over her feelings of worry in one weighty arena of life. Certainly, she could do it again.

Worries about the family financial condition continued to plague her. She described her financial concerns as the number one source of worry in her life. She reaffirmed the fact that she didn't care about being rich, but just wanted to be able to make ends meet. This is a particularly problematic area for both Allison and her husband. Whenever she mentions her worry about money, her husband becomes a bit defensive. He acts as though she thinks he is not able to provide for her.

To relieve some of the stress over money and her husband's response, I explained that one of the significant needs for many women is to have a sense of security. Most female concerns about money revolve around the need to feel secure. Men can be different; males often think of money as a scoreboard. Their thoughts

tend to revolve around the desire for prestige and the peer acknowl-
edgment that money can provide. I further explained that most
financial questions directed to a husband by a wife would be met
defensively. Many males would interpret such questions as doubting their ability to provide. While a woman's monetary needs can
circle around the issue of security, a man's financial needs often
orbit around his ego. That's why a husband can get defensive. Defining these differing roles helped her to relax.

We spent the rest of session three going through Luke 21 and
Philippians 8–9 as described in chapter four of this book. We then
reviewed the "Faith is the oil in the machinery of life, worry is the
sand" concept. We also reviewed the key words associated with
the Philippians 4 passage. Following a review of where we had
been, I set out to explain the coping strategy as described in chapter four. She was to select three key verses, write them on 3–inch
by 5–inch cards, and begin to memorize them. She agreed to review
the cards several times a day and to tie their review to some form
of ritual. I suggested that she review them at every red light, coffee break, or something of that nature.

As I explained how to take every thought captive and make it
obedient to Christ, Allison perked up. She was beginning to see
that there was something concrete that she could do instead of
worry. She left the office that day with her hope renewed. My hope
was that she would experience a week filled with victories.

Session Four

As Allison entered the office today, there was a pronounced difference in her attitude. Rather than being jovial and nervous, she
was contemplative. Her spirit wasn't depressive, but reflective. She
gave the impression that she was serious about dealing with her
worry. This week had gone much better than the previous week.
There were some real bright spots. One night she woke up terribly
worried about something. Rather than toss and turn, she began to
review the verses she had committed to memory. Her story was
very encouraging. She was illustrating her understanding of the
"taking every thought captive" concept. Within a few minutes she
fell asleep again, and remained asleep for the rest of the night. I

asked what she had been worried about; her response, "That's the funny thing, I can't remember. This stuff must be working, huh?"

Allison had memorized 1 Peter 5:7, Philippians 4:6–8, and was working on 1 John 5 and Psalm 94. She was reviewing the verses over coffee in the morning and then during her coffee breaks at work. She also concluded her day with a quiet time that included reviewing her verses. It was obvious that these verses were becoming very much a part of her thought process.

I asked how she was feeling about worry, and commented that she seemed more relaxed. She said that during the past week or so, she had noticed that the feelings of tension would come and go. She viewed this as very positive. Prior to Strategic Pastoral Counseling, she was tense most of the time. Just being able to notice worried tension coming meant that it hadn't been there all the time!

Another encouraging piece of information surfaced. Her husband had received an excellent inquiry concerning a job offer. While the contract wasn't on the table, it might certainly be an answer to their financial worries. The downside was that she would have to uproot and relocate the family. She was really involved in her local church and wasn't too anxious to leave the community. The two of them were facing a major life-change decision. Normally such an opportunity would have sent her spinning with the "What if's" of worry. I asked, "How do you feel?" She said, "Amazingly enough, I've been handling this one pretty well." Once again, this was progress.

This session's focus was on action. As we read through James 2, Luke 21, and James 4 (as quoted in chapter five), she became a bit troubled. "Taking action has never been easy for me," she said. Following a few minutes of dialogue, she came to the conclusion that her habit of inactivity was due to the uncomfortable feeling of failing to meet her expectations. Flat out failure was equally hard to accept; therefore, inactivity was more comfortable emotionally. I told her that allowing worry to paralyze her and failing to act simply allowed others to make her choices for her. She agreed.

I explained the parable of the talents to illustrate the absolute necessity of action. God was able to bless the first two servants because they acted. The third, however, God was unable to bless since he had buried his talent. He had failed to act. God can't bless inactivity. The formula is simple: nothing plus nothing equals nothing.

Allison felt as though she could begin to take action because her feelings of worry and worrisome thoughts were being countered by prayer and by guarding her perspective. I explained how to develop an action plan. Using the potential of a job change and moving as an example, I walked through how she and her husband might begin taking action a step at a time. Since taking action was such a problem for both her and her husband, I asked her to tell me how they might develop an action plan. With a few minor corrections and additional thoughts, she left the office with the assignment to continue memorizing verses, praying about worrisome issues, and guarding her perspective. In addition, she was to develop an action plan with her husband to help them act upon the job opportunity, rather than worry.

Session Five

We began session five talking about the most troublesome issues associated with Allison's worry. She said that the most difficult step thus far for her had been the action step. She had seen excellent progress with her worrisome feelings. She was thrilled with the strides she had made with her thoughts of worry. She related several instances where she had defeated worrisome thoughts by countering them with Scripture. However, taking action has always been, and still is, very difficult. We reviewed together the action steps from our previous session and talked through the five questions from chapter six. Our review seemed to help clarify the thoughts behind the questions. Hearing them restated and illustrated was very helpful.

Another area of difficulty for Allison was the arena of guilt. She was presently feeling more guilt now than before we started counseling. Allison has strong perfectionist tendencies that often leave her guilt-ridden. While she knows God is gracious and forgiving, her greater understanding of the Scripture's prohibition to worry has increased her sense of guilt. To offset those guilty feelings we discussed Isaiah 43:25, Psalm 103:3–4, Micah 7:19, Psalm 103:12, and Isaiah 38:17. Allison found comfort in the verses. We determined that they should be the next group of Scriptures to commit to her memory. I pointed out that the best way to deal with her guilty feelings was to memorize the Scriptures and confront her feelings of guilt with the truth of the Scriptures. The concept is identical to what she had already done with her worrisome feelings.

Our final session together included a review of Matthew 6:25–34. I explained the vastly different culture to which Jesus was speaking, and explained the rational reasons for first-century people to worry about food, clothing, and health. Despite logical and reasonable reasons for worry, worry was still forbidden. Since two of the major areas of Allison's worry related to health and finances, this passage was especially fitting for our final session together. Our concluding minutes together were very positive. Allison conveyed the monumental leap forward she had taken in dealing with her worry. She is the kind of person who finds motivation to do more when she is able to see tangible results. The past two weeks had included such positive strides forward that Allison was certain that she would be able to continue. We concluded our time together with a brief conversation about informal contacts in the future. I explained that she need not feel apprehensive or self-conscious whenever our paths might cross. I certainly did not think of her as Allison, the worrier, but would always view her as a courageous lady who was willing to confront her fears.

Concluding Thoughts

As a pastor, I found the five-step progression to be delightfully productive. The limited time frame kept us focused. Having a specific purpose behind each session kept us moving forward. Each session built nicely upon the previous one. Review was simple and productive. Allison's progress was obvious; I couldn't have been more surprised or pleased. No doubt, her progress was due to her desire and willingness to work so hard.

Annotated Bibliography

*T*he following important books on worry are arranged in chronological order by the date of their publication to help illustrate how approaches to worry have changed over the last 60 years.

Chappell, M. N. 1938. *In the name of common sense: Worry and its control.* New York: Macmillan.

    Chappell sought to help people with worry, an activity that he called a "perverted use of the human brain." The author believed that worry was learned by practice and that it could be forgotten if only people would stop doing it. The author's approach shares many features with more recent titles: I must recognize that the problem is in me, not in someone else; I'll change what I can in the environment and then adapt to the rest. But the book differs from current approaches by advocating that worriers totally avoid their worrisome thoughts: I must discuss my worries only with my physician, and I must discourage others from ever reminding me of my worries.

Carnegie, D. 1944. *How to stop worrying and start living.* New York: Simon and Schuster.

    Dale Carnegie's classic book, his second most famous, has seen many revisions and has sold millions of copies. This title reflects the early wave of self-help books and consists mainly of uplifting stories of people who have overcome their worry habits. The book is broader in its coverage than just worry. Carnegie did not worry if his book was inconsistent at times. If inspiration and enthusiastic testimonials alone could cure worry, this book would be all that the worrier needs.

Fischer, W. F. 1970. *Theories of anxiety.* New York: Harper and Row.

    An early attempt to survey all the various psychological theories regarding anxiety. Fischer then seeks to integrate them by synthesizing the common elements among these theories.

Hauck, P. A. 1975. *Overcoming worry and fear.* Philadelphia: Westminster Press.

A psychological treatment for laypersons. Hauck feels that fear and anxiety are similar (except that in anxiety you do not know the object of your fear), and that worry is the cognitive aspect of fear—only implicitly Christian.

McFadden, J. 1983. *The fear factor*. Ann Arbor: Servant Books.

Written from a pastoral perspective, this psychologically-informed book provides us with a comprehensive review of scriptural teaching about worry. He feels that the marks of a Christian (confidence, boldness, and courage) are the antidotes to worry that besets the believer.

Hart, A. D. 1989. *Overcoming anxiety*. Dallas: Word.

This comprehensive title deals with worry and its attendant conditions from a psychological and biblical standpoint. Hart describes the anxiety that is addressed in Scripture as "worry anxiety." Hart is convinced that our faith gives us resources to combat worry, a mental activity that is "uniformly condemned by Scripture." Hart also sees anxiety as an outgrowth of fear.

Rapee, R. M. and Barlow, D. H. (eds.) 1991. *Chronic anxiety*. New York: Guilford.

This edited volume contains state-of-the-art thinking about worry. Secular in its orientation, this book will give the serious reader updates on current research and theorizing about the common human bedevilment called worry. Rapee and Barlow fairly represent all the major centers for the study of worry in the English-speaking world.

Backus, W. 1991. *The good news about worry*. Minneapolis: Bethany House.

Backus uses cognitive-behavioral theory integrated with his biblical faith to write this helpful volume on worry. The book contains many case studies of how clients can use their faith to reduce the intrusion of worry into their daily functioning. Backus's goal is to help people reduce their worry, not eliminate it. He feels that worry is based upon misbeliefs that can be combatted with beliefs from God's word. Useful for counselors and counselees alike. Backus has given us a very hopeful book on worry.

Craske, M. G., Barlow, D. H. and O'Leary, T. 1992. *Mastery of your anxiety and worry*. Albany: Graywind Publications.

This set of self-help materials reflects the pioneering work of the Center for Stress and Anxiety Disorders at the State University of New York at Albany. Their materials are secular but helpful for the Christian as well. Included are a workbook for the client and a set of monitoring forms and worry records. The materials systematically help the worrier master the habit patterns that keep their worry behaviors firmly in place. Cost for one set: $19.95. Available from:

Graywind Publications
c/o 1535 Western Avenue
Albany, New York 12203

Reference List

Benner, D. G. 1992. *Strategic pastoral counseling*. Grand Rapids: Baker.

Bing, S. 1989. Don't worry, keep busy. *Esquire* Nov., 99–101.

Bunyan, J. 1675. *Pilgrim's progress*. New York: A. L. Brent.

Hauck, P. A. 1975. *Overcoming worry and fear*. Philadelphia: Westminster.

Henry, C. F. H. 1987. An eye on the cradle. *Christianity Today, 31* Nov. 6, 26–7.

Malony, H. N. 1988. The clinical assessment of optimal religious functioning. *Review of Religious Research, 30* (1), 3–17.

Rice, J. R. 1948. *God's cure for anxious care*. Wheaton: Sword of the Lord.